JUST *Jazz* REAL BOOK

190 "Invitation"

228 Lush Life

Project Manager: AARON STANG
Project Consultants: BILL GALLIFORD, ETHAN NEUBURG and PETE BARENBREGGE
Music Arranging, Engraving and Project Management:
ARTEMIS MUSIC LIMITED, Pinewood Studios, Iver Heath, Bucks, SL0 0NH, UK
www.artemismusic.com
US Arranging Supervisor: BILL GALLIFORD
Music Editors: BILL GALLIFORD and ETHAN NEUBURG
US Production Coordinator: SHARON MARLOW
Text Editor: NADINE DeMARCO
Discography Research: AARON STANG and DONNA SALZBURG
Copyright Clearance and Licensing: DAVE OLSEN and SHARON HARRIS
Art Design: CARMEN FORTUNATO

How to use this fakebook

HOW TO USE THIS FAKEBOOK

Over the last several years, fakebooks have evolved from those "under-the-counter," unauthorized (and many times illegal) publications to often elaborately produced books that cover a wide range of musical genres. From their inception, fakebooks were designed to provide professional musicians with a cheat-sheet style of arrangement, where they could see the skeletal elements of a song in a brief single- or half-page format. But these early books were of poor print quality, were often mistake-ridden, and were sometimes filled with questionable song material. In the 1970s, the name of one particular fakebook was echoed across the professional music landscape: *The Real Book* began to change the face of fakebook publications. The arrangements were much more clearly presented; the chord symbols, melody lines, and general musical content were just as the working professional musician would play. Size and quality of print was improved, and the song selection was extremely appropriate. It set the standard for fakebooks. Only one problem: it was still an unauthorized publication. Thus, the stage was set for the music publishing world to develop and produce professional-quality, legal fakebooks.

The book you hold in your hands was designed to be an indispensable resource. Every effort has been made to provide **the best song material**—which is useful and applicable to the designated song genres throughout this series; **the best arrangements**—utilizing the skills of professional musicians across continents *(we did extensive research from existing print and recorded sources for every song, combined with the musical expertise of musicians around the globe to come up with the most commonly distilled arrangements)*; and **the finest quality of print**—easy to read from a reasonable distance and featuring a sharp, professional calligraphy print style.

What follows are some general guidelines describing our approach to developing these arrangements:

FORM & FORMAT

Verse/Chorus Designations: The most familiar portions of most of the songs in this collection are the *Chorus* sections, sometimes referred to as *Refrain* or *Head*. Many also included *Verses,* which are not as readily known. Whenever possible, we've tried to provide the *Verse* sections of each song, and have designated them accordingly.
Key Signatures: They can be found on the first music line, or system of each page only, or where any change of key might occur. You should assume that key applies throughout the song unless otherwise noted.
Rehearsal Letters: We've placed rehearsal letters at logical phrase breaks throughout the *Chorus* or main section of each song: [A] [B], etc.

Repeats, Endings: Traditional repeat markings are to be followed as usual. Endings are clearly numbered and indicate the total number of times they are to be played through. *(For solos, which are not accounted for in the form, we suggest you use the first endings and repeat as necessary.)*
Form Indicators: The following indicators are used throughout this book: D.C.; D.S.𝄋; D.C. al Coda; D.S.𝄋 al Coda; 𝄌 Coda; To Coda 𝄌

Optional D.C.: Some of the *Verse* sections contain more than one lyric line. It was a common practice in early piano/vocal sheet music to use repeats for the *Chorus* or *Refrain* sections only presumably because that represented the **main** song. The form did not take you back to the *Verse* section, effectively making the second lyric line optional. We've added the **Optional D.C.** indication within the first endings of the *Chorus* sections on a few songs where this instance applies. This simply gives the performer the option of going back to the beginning of the song (D.C.) to use the second lyric.

Added Music Staves: We have included some additional material on certain songs to capture commonly recognized intros, endings, riffs, and other nuances from classic performances. These additional staves often accommodate a piano part, bass line, or other commonly identifiable instrumental line. We've made these sections brief and concise, allowing the general intention to apply throughout the song.

Instrumental Cue Notes: Cue notes are used on particular instrumental parts to differentiate from the main melody, or primary melodic lines. For instance, if a song contains an intro with a distinctive bass part, we've put that bass part in cues. Any secondary instrumental lines, whether acting as support of a melody or acting as a counter-melody, are usually indicated in cues as well. Harmony notes are also in cues.

Improvised Solo Sections: We've indicated throughout these arrangements where improvised solos are commonly played. Usually, the directions are included in the form directives: (AD LIB. SOLOS ON SECTIONS A & B), etc. And in some cases there are sections provided that include a stave with slash notation and a set of chord symbols.

Ex.

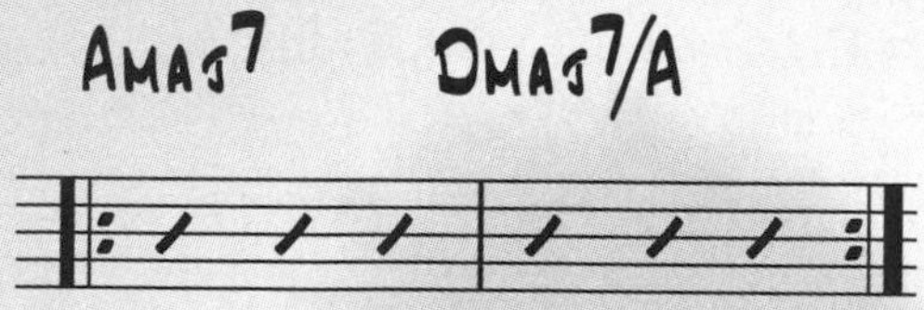

Rhythmic Notation: Rhythmic slashes are used in specific instances to reflect drum patterns or common band hits.

Ex.

Alternate Song Versions: Two songs within this collection have alternate versions: "Blue Train" shows the original recorded version by John Coltrane—this is a **dominant key** version—and the second is a **minor key** version, which is probably the most familiar of the two. "Cast Your Fate to the Wind " shows the **instrumental** version popularized by Vince Guaraldi plus a **lyric** version. *(There were significant melodic differences between the two versions, so we provided both for clarity.)*

Alternate Song Sections: Some songs include alternate versions of particular song sections. They are usually placed at the end of the song, with specific instructions regarding content. These often reflect either different well-known versions or differences in the composer's original intent and how it is commonly performed.

CHORDS

Main & Alternate Substitution Labeling: The chord symbols found directly above the melody line are what we consider the **main** chords. These chord choices are derived from either original changes found in the most reliable piano/vocal sources, from the most famous recorded sources, from notes or arrangements by the composers themselves, or from the most commonly known renditions typically played by professional musicians. We have also provided some **alternate substitutions**, which are shown in parentheses above the **main** symbols. These changes are derived from either selected popular recordings by artists highly identified with a particular song or are based on common alternate renderings. These chords are optional and may be either played in place of or in conjunction with the **main** symbols. Notice that these chords will last as long as the **main** symbols or until the closing parenthesis is indicated.

Chord Labeling: Chords are labeled clearly according to their appropriate function. For instance, major triads will, of course, be identified by the appropriate letter name: C; B; ETC. Minor chords will simply include a lowercase M after each letter identifier: CM; AM; ETC. Minor 7th, major 7th, dominant 7th, and diminished 7th chords follow the same course: CM7; CMAJ7; C7; CDIM7; ETC. Any altered chord tones are put in parentheses: C7(♭5); CM7(♭5); C7(♭9/♭5); ETC.

LYRICS

We've clearly punctuated lyrics to each song to maintain proper sentence structure.

Contents

Appendices:

Composer Index

Composers are listed last name first. When two or more composers are listed, the music composer is listed first, followed by the lyricist.

Miles Davis, 1982
Courtesy of Chuck Pulin, Star File, Inc.

500 MILES HIGH

MED. LATIN

WORDS & MUSIC BY
CHICK COREA AND NEVILLE POTTER

AIN'T MISBEHAVIN'

MUSIC BY THOMAS "FATS" WALLER AND HARRY BROOKS
WORDS BY ANDY RAZAF

A FELICIDADE

(A/K/A ADIEU TRISTESSE)

MEDIUM BOSSA/ SAMBA

WORDS AND MUSIC BY VINICIUS DE MORAES,
ANDRE SALVET, AND ANTONIO CARLOS JOBIM

D
CMAJ9
(F7 CMAJ9)
A fe - li - ci - da - de do po - bre pa - re - ce
A fe - li - ci - da - de esta so - nhan - do
GM7 C9
A grande ilusão do carnaval.
Nos olhos da minha namorada.
FMAJ7 DM7
A gente trabalha o ano inteiro Por um momento de sonho Pra fazer a fantasia
É como esta noite, passando, passando Em busca da madrugada Falem baixo por favor
G7 C6/9
F#M7(b5) B7(b9) EM7 A7(#5)
DM7 (G#DIM7) G7(b9)
E
AM7 AM7/G
a De rei ou de pirata ou jardineira.
Pra que ela acorde alegre com o dia
(D7 DM7)
D7/F# DM7/F AM7
Pra tudo se acabar na quarta feira.
Oferecendo beijos de amor.
(D9)
BM7(b5) E7(#5)
1 AM7
2. Tris - te -
2 AM7

AIR CONDITIONING

MEDIUM BLUES

BY CHARLIE PARKER

AIREGIN

MUSIC BY SONNY ROLLINS

BRIGHT SWING
A
FM
C7(#9 b5)
FM
(F7(#9))
F7
BbM
F7(#9 #5)
BbM7
(Bb7)
B
1
(DM7
G7)
DM7
G7
CMAJ7
C#M7
F#7
BMAJ7
CM7
F7
BbMAJ7
BbM7
Eb7
AbMAJ7
GM7(b5)
C7
C
2
(Eb7
CDIM7
F7(#9))
Eb7
AbMAJ7
CM7(b5)
F7
(Eb7
GM7(b5)
C7(#9))
D.C. FOR SOLOS
BbM7
Eb7(b9)
Ab
FINE LAST TIME
SOLO BREAK

AJA

Words and Music by
Walter Becker and Donald Fagen

D
SOLO SECTION
A G A G A G A G
A G A G F G F F#M11
G CMAJ7
E7SUS F# G A G F#M11 G/F FMAJ7 G
1
D.S.
2
G/F FMAJ7 EM/G FMAJ7 CM11 BM11
E
Bb/C B/C# E/F# Eb/F D/E C#/D# D/E C#/D# E/F#
1
EM/G FMAJ7 CM11 BM11
2
C#MAJ7(b5) CMAJ7(b5)
D.C. AL CODA
CODA BM11
REPEAT AD LIB. AND FADE

ALICE IN WONDERLAND

JAZZ WALTZ

MUSIC BY SAMMY FAIN
WORDS BY BOB HILLIARD

* CUES REFLECT BILL EVANS RENDITION. HE USUALLY PLAYED SECTIONS A AND C ONE OCTAVE HIGHER

ANTHROPOLOGY

BY CHARLIE PARKER & DIZZY GILLESPIE

UP-TEMPO BE-BOP

ALL MY TOMORROWS

LYRIC BY SAMMY CAHN
MUSIC BY JAMES VAN HEUSEN

Cm7 F9 Gmaj7 Em7 Em7/D C#m7(b5) Cm6
bet - ter than I that luck keeps pass - ing me by, that's fate!
G6/B Em7 Am7 D13(b9) B7(#9/#5) E9sus E7(b9)
But with you there at my side, I'll soon be turn - ing the tide, just
C
Am7 D7 E7(b9) Am9 Am7(b5) D7(b9)
wait! As long as I've got arms that cling at all, it's
(Bm7)
Gmaj9 E-7 Bbdim7 Am7 D9sus D7/C
you that I'll be cling - ing to. And all the dreams I dream, beg, or
Bm7 E7(b9) E7 Am7 D7(b9) F9(#11) E7
bor - row, on some bright to - mor - row, they'll all come true. And
1
Am9 Cm/Eb D7(b9) G E7(b9) E7
all my bright to - mor - rows be - long to you! To -
2
Am9 D9 Cm7 D7 G Cm6 G6/9
all my bright to - mor - rows be - long to you!

OH, LADY BE GOOD

MUSIC AND LYRICS BY
GEORGE GERSHWIN
AND IRA GERSHWIN

FREELY
VERSE:
EM F#M11 B7 GMAJ7 (EM/G) AM9 EM/B B7SUS B7(#5) EM6
Lis - ten to my tale of woe; it's ter - ri - bly sad, but true.
Au - burn and bru - nette and blonde, I love 'em all, tall or small.
G AM11 D7 G/B CMAJ7 G/D D7SUS D13 G6
All dressed up, no place to go; each eve - ning I'm aw - f'ly blue.
But some - how they don't grow fond; they stag - ger, but nev - er fall.
D7 G D7 G B7
I must win some win - some miss; can't go on like this.
Win - ter's gone, and now it's Spring! Love, where is thy sting?
E F#M11 B7 E/G# AMAJ9 (AM9) E/B B7SUS B13 E D7/F#
I could blos - som out, I know, with some-bod - y just like you, so...
If some - bod - y won't re - spond, I'm go - ing to end it all, so...
A BALLAD/MED. SWING
CHORUS:
G6 C9 G6 G#DIM7 (C9 BM7 E7(b9))
Oh, sweet and love - ly la - dy, be good! Oh,
Oh, sweet and love - ly la - dy, be good! Oh,
D7/A (AM7 D7(b9)) D7 D13 G6 EM7 AM7 D7(b9)
la - dy, be good to me!
la - dy, be good to me!

(C9 Bm7 E7(b9))
G6 C9 G6 Gdim7
I am so aw - f'ly mis - un - der - stood, so,
I am so aw - f'ly mis - un - der - stood, so,
(Am7 D7(b9))
D7/A D7 D13 G6 Dm7 G7
la - dy, be good to me.
la - dy, be good to me.
B
(C#dim7 G/D) (F#m7(b5) B7(b9))
C6 D9 C/G G G6 D7
Oh, please have some pit - y;
This is tu - lip weath - er,
(Am9)
Em7 A9 D11 D13
I'm all a - lone in this big cit - y. I tell you,
so let's put two and two to - geth - er. I tell you,
C
(C9 Bm7 E7(b9))
G6 C9 G6 G#dim7
I'm just a lone - some babe in the wood, so,
I'm just a lone - some babe in the wood, so,
(Am7 D7(b9))
D7/A D7 D13 1 G6 E7(b9)
la - dy, be good to me!
la - dy, be good to
Am7 D7(b9) (OPTIONAL D.C.) 2 G6 C9 G6/9
me!

ALL THE THINGS YOU ARE

MUSIC BY JEROME KERN
WORDS BY OSCAR HAMMERSTEIN II

(Cm7 Gb7(#11) Fm7 B7(#11) Bb7 E7(#11) EbMaj7 A7(#11))
Cm7 Fm7 Bb7 EbMaj7
You are the breath-less hush of eve-ning that
AbMaj7 Am7(b5) D7 (B/G G6) GMaj7
trem-bles on the brink of a love-ly song. You are the
B
Am7 D7 GMaj7
an-gel glow that lights a star, the dear-est
F#m7(b5) B7 EMaj7 C7alt C+
things I know are what you are.
whole tone clusters
C
(Fm7 B7(#11) Bbm7 E7(#11) Eb7 A7(#11))
Fm7 Bbm7 Eb7 AbMaj7
Some day my hap-py arms will hold you and
(DbMaj7 Gb7)
DbMaj7 Dbm9 Gb7 Cm7 Bdim7
D6 13
some day I'll know that mo-ment di-vine when
Bbm7 Eb9 Ab6 Gm7(b5) C7alt Ab6
all the things you are are mine. mine.

ALONE TOGETHER

BALLAD OR MEDIUM SWING

WORDS BY HOWARD DIETZ
MUSIC BY ARTHUR SCHWARTZ

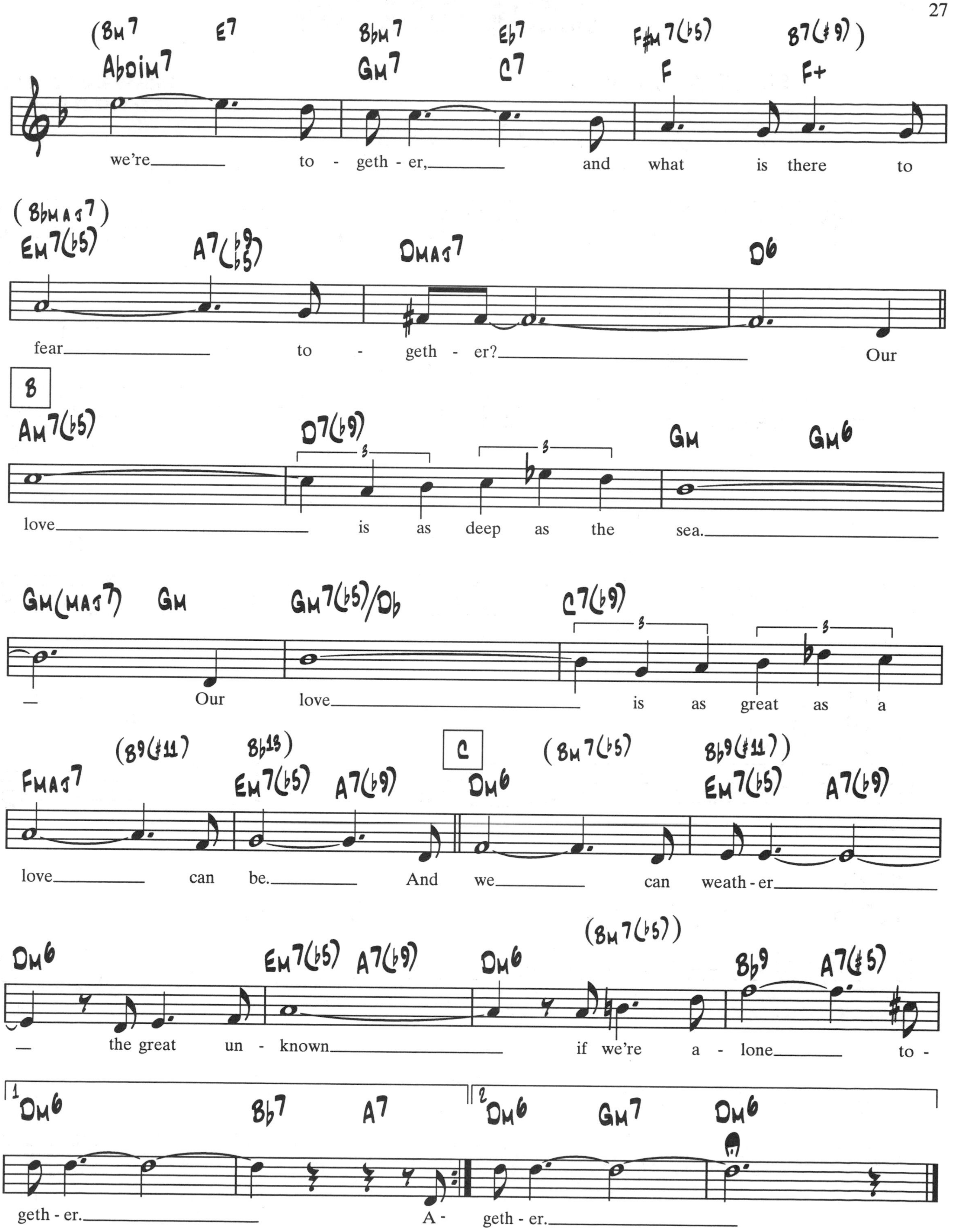
(Bm7 E7 B♭m7 E♭7 F♯m7(♭5) B7(♯9))
A♭dim7 Gm7 C7 F F+
we're to - geth - er, and what is there to
(B♭maj7)
Em7(♭5) A7(♭9/♭5) Dmaj7 D6
fear to - geth - er? Our
8
Am7(♭5) D7(♭9) Gm Gm6
love is as deep as the sea.
Gm(maj7) Gm Gm7(♭5)/D♭ C7(♭9)
Our love is as great as a
(B9(♯11) B♭13) (Bm7(♭5) B♭9(♯11))
Fmaj7 Em7(♭5) A7(♭9) Dm6 Em7(♭5) A7(♭9)
C
love can be. And we can weath - er
(Bm7(♭5))
Dm6 Em7(♭5) A7(♭9) Dm6 B♭9 A7(♯5)
the great un - known if we're a - lone to -
1 Dm6 B♭7 A7
2 Dm6 Gm7 Dm6
geth - er. A - geth - er.

ANA MARIA

MEDIUM BOSSA-NOVA

BY WAYNE SHORTER

G7(b9)SUS
EbMAJ9/G
G7(b9)SUS
EbMAJ9/G
A
GMAJ7
Eb(9)/G
G13SUS
Eb(9)/G
DbMAJ7/F
GbMAJ7(#11)
AbM7
Bb/Ab
GM7
C9SUS
D/C
C9SUS
Ab(9)/C
G7(b9)SUS
EbMAJ9/G
G7(b9)SUS
EbMAJ9/G
B
GMAJ7
G13SUS
Eb/F
E7(#9 b5)
Eb9SUS

DMAJ7 F7(#5) BbM9 AbM7 Bb/Ab
GM7 C9SUS BbMAJ7 AM7 FM9
Bb9SUS Db13SUS
C
BM9 EbM11 EbM7
DMAJ7 F7(#5) BbM9 AbM7 Bb/Ab
GM7 C9SUS BbMAJ7 AM7 FM9 EM7 G7(b9)
D
VAMP, SOLOS & FADE
EbMAJ9/G G7(b9)SUS EbMAJ9/G G7(b9)SUS EbMAJ9/G

ARMAGEDDON

BY WAYNE SHORTER

MEDIUM SWING

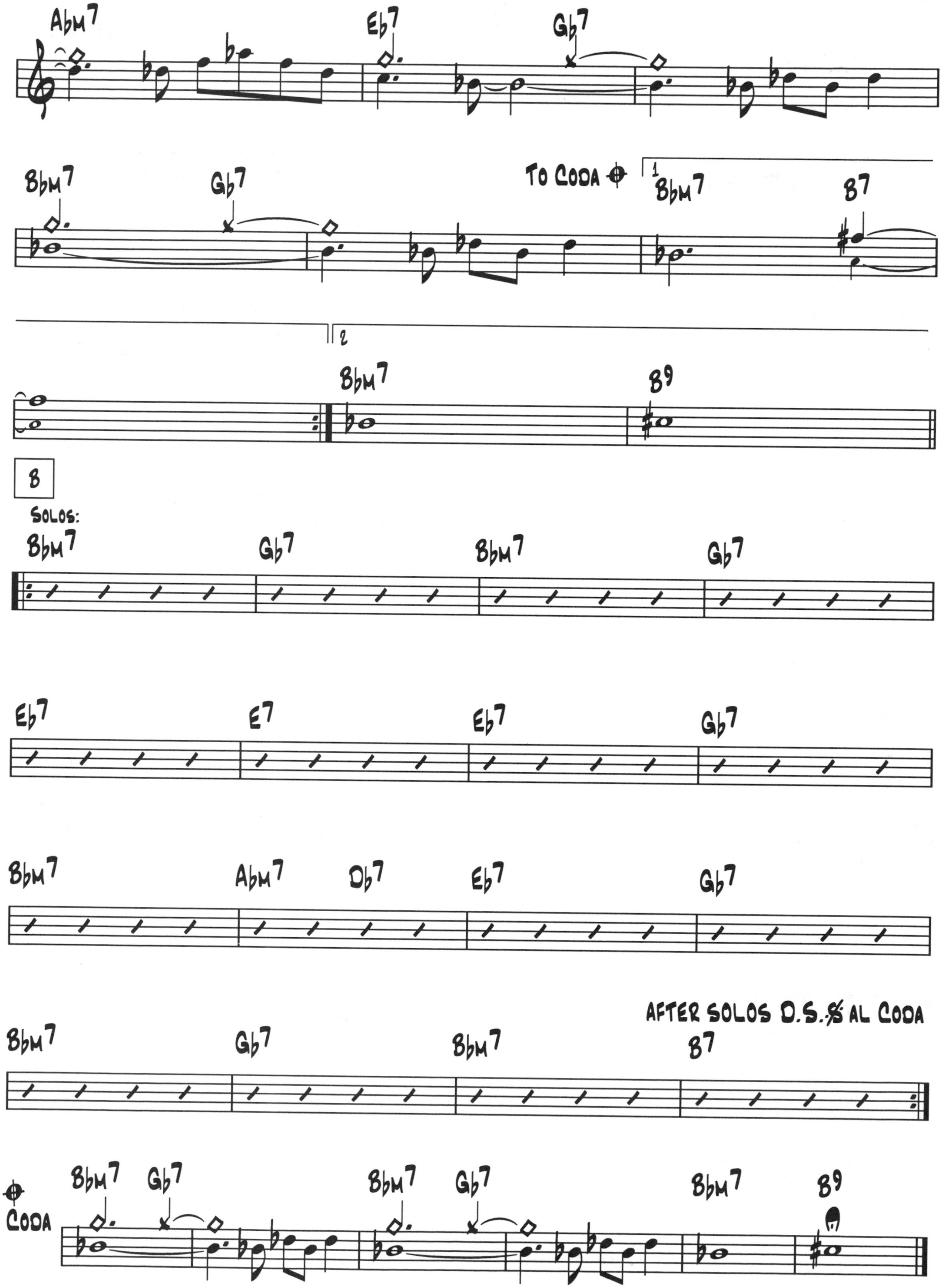
AbM7
Eb7
Gb7
BbM7
Gb7
TO CODA
1
BbM7
B7
2
BbM7
B9
8
SOLOS:
BbM7
Gb7
BbM7
Gb7
Eb7
E7
Eb7
Gb7
BbM7
AbM7
Db7
Eb7
Gb7
AFTER SOLOS D.S. AL CODA
BbM7
Gb7
BbM7
B7
CODA
BbM7
Gb7
BbM7
Gb7
BbM7
B9

AS TIME GOES BY

WORDS AND MUSIC BY HERMAN HUPFELD

FREELY OR BALLAD
VERSE:
EbMAJ7 CM7 FM7 Bb7
This day and age we're liv - ing in gives cause for ap - re - hen-sion, with
EbMAJ7 Eb6 GM7 C7(b9) FM7 Bb7
speed and new in - ven - tion, and things like third di - men - sion. Yet, we grow a tri - fle wear - y, with
EbMAJ7 CM7 Bb6/F D7(b9) GM7 GbDIM7 FM7 Bb7
Mis-ter Ein-stein's the-'ry, so we must get down to earth, at times re - lax, re - lieve the ten - sion. No
FM7 Bb7 GM7 CM7
mat - ter what the pro - gress or what may yet be proved, the
Db13 E13
FM7 Ab/C AbM6/Cb Bb7 C7(b9)
sim - ple facts of life are such they can - not be re - moved. You
A CHORUS:
(GM7(b5) C7(b9) Abm7 Db9)
FM7 Bb7 BbM6 FM7 Bb7(b9) EbMAJ7 FM7
must re - mem - ber this, a kiss is still a kiss, a sigh is just a sigh;
Bb7
(F#DIM7)
GM7 CM7 F7 FM7 Bb7SUS Bb7(b9) EbMAJ7 AbMAJ7 GM7 C7(b9)
the fun-da-men-tal things ap - ply, as time goes by. And
D9

when two lov-ers woo, they still say, 'I love you,' on that you can re - ly; no
mat - ter what the fu - ture brings, as time goes by.
B
Moon-light and love songs nev - er out of date, hearts full of pas - sion,
jea - lous - y and hate; wom - an needs man and
man must have his mate, that no man can de - ny. It's
C
still the same old sto - ry, a fight for love and glo - ry, a
case of do or die! The world will al - ways wel - come
lov - ers as time goes by. You by.

Charlie Parker
Courtesy of Star File, Inc.

AU PRIVAVE

BY CHARLIE PARKER

MEDIUM SWING
F
GM7
C7
F
GM7
CM7
F7(#5)
Bb7(b9)
BbM7
Eb7
F
GM7
AM7
D7(b9)
(C7)
GM7
C7
F
D7(b9)
1
GM7
C7
2
GM7
C13

AUTUMN IN NEW YORK

WORDS AND MUSIC BY VERNON DUKE

FREELY
VERSE:
GM7 C7 AM7 F C7(b5) C7
It's time to end my lone-ly hol-i-day and bid the coun-try a has-ty fare-
FM6 GM7 C7 AM7 BOIM7 Ab/Eb G/Eb
well. So on this grey and mel-an-chol-y day I'll move to a Man-hat-tan ho-
Ab/Eb BbM11 Eb9 Ab6/9 Bb9 Eb7(b9/#5)
tel. I'll dis-pose of my rose-col-oured chat-tels and pre-pare for my share of ad-
CM7(b5) C7SUS C7 F6 GM7(b5) F6/9
ven-tures and bat-tles. Here on the twen-ty sev-enth floor, look-ing
GM7(b5) Db7 C7(#5) F6 AM7 D7(b9)
down on the ci-ty I hate and a-dore!
A
BALLAD
CHORUS:
GM7 AM7 BbMAJ7 C13 FMAJ7 GM7
Au-tumn in New York, why does it seem so in-vit-ing?
Au-tumn in New York, the gleam-ing roof-tops at sun-down.
AM7 D7(b9) GM7 AM7 BbMAJ7 C13
Au-tumn in New York, it spells the thrill of first
Au-tumn in New York, it lifts you up when you're

Am7(b5) D7(b9) Gm7
night - ing, glit - ter - ing crowds and
run down, jad - ed rou - és and
Bbm7 Eb7 Abmaj7 Dm7(b5)
shim - mer - ing clouds in can - yons of steel, they're
gay di - vor - cees who lunch at the Ritz, will
Cm7 Am7(b5) Dm7(b5) G13 Cmaj7 Gm7 C7 C7(#5)
mak - ing me feel I'm home. It's
tell you that 'it's di - vine!' This
8
Gm7 Am7 Bbmaj7 C13 Fmaj7 Gm7 Am7 D9 Dm7 Dbm7
Au - tumn in New York, that brings the prom - ise of new love.
Au - tumn in New York, trans - forms the slums in - to May - fair.
Cm9 Dm7 Ebm6 (Gb7 F7) F7(#5) Bbm Gb7
Au - tumn in New York is of - ten min - gled with pain.
Au - tumn in New York, you'll need no cas - tles in Spain.
Fm C7(#5) Fm Ab13 Dbmaj7 Ab13
Dream - ers with emp - ty hands may sigh for ex - ot - ic
Lov - ers that bless the dark on bench - es in Cen - tral
Dbmaj7 Ab7 Gm7 Am7 Bbm6 (Db7 C7) C7(#5)
lands; it's Au - tumn in New York, it's good to live it a -
Park, greet Au - tumn in New York, it's good to live it a -
1 Fm Ab13
gain.
2 Fm
gain.

AZURE

Words & Music by
Duke Ellington and Irving Mills

BERNIE'S TUNE

BY BERNIE MILLER

MEDIUM SWING

A
DM
Bb9(#11)
EM7(b5)
A7
DM
1
EM7(b5) A7
2
B
Bb6 GM7 CM7 F7 Bb6 GM7 CM7 F7
Bb6 GM7 CM7 F7 Bb6 EM7(b5) A7
C
DM
Bb9(#11)
EM7(b5)
A7
DM
1
EM7(b5) A7
2

BE BOP

BY JOHN "DIZZY" GILLESPIE

Ebm7
Ab7(#9)
DbMAJ7
Gm7(b5)
C7(b5)
C
Fm
Gm7(b5)
Fm/Ab
Bbm6
Fm/C
Gm7(b5)
C7
Fm
Gm7(b5)
Fm/Ab
Bbm6
Fm/C
1
D.S.𝄋 FOR SOLOS
2 (LAST TIME)
Gm7(b5) C7
Fm
Gm7(b5) C7
Fm
N.C.
C7(b5)

BEYOND THE SEA

Words & Music by
Charles Trenet & Jack Lawrence
Moderately
F Dm7 Gm7 C7 F Dm7 Gm7 C7
1. Some - where
A
F Dm7 Gm7 C7 F Dm7 Gm7 C7
be-yond the sea, some - where, wait - ing for me,
F A7 Dm7 C7 F Dm7
my lov - er stands on Tom - my
Bb6 D7/A Gm7 C7 Dm7 Bb Dm/A G G7
Sands, watch - ing the ships that go sail - ing,
C7
sail-ing. (2.) Some - where
(3.)
B
F Dm7 Gm7 C7 F Dm7
be-yond the sea, she's there
be-yond the shore, we're gon-na kiss
Gm7 C7 F A7 Dm7 C7
wait - ing for me. If I could fly
just as be - fore. And hap - py we'll
F Dm7 Bb6 D7/A Gm7 C7
like birds on high, then straight to her arms
be be - yond the sea, and nev - er a - gain

DM7 Bb GM7 C7 F6/9 E7 C A F#M7
– I'd go sail - ing.
– will I go sail - ing. It is far
BM7 E7 A F#M7 BM7 E7 A
be-yond the star, it is near beyond the moon.
G7 D C AM7 DM7 G7 C AM7
I know be-yond a doubt, uh, my
DM7 G7 C6 1 GM7 C7 2 C7SUS C7
heart will lead me there. 3. Soon we will meet we will
F DM7 GM7 C7 F DM7
meet, I know we'll meet, be-yond the shore, we're gon - na kiss
GM7 C7 F A7 DM7 C7
just as be - fore. And hap - py we'll
F DM7 Bb6 D7/A GM7 C7
be be - yond the sea, while nev - er a - gain
DM7 Bb G C7 F DM7
will I go sail - ing. (No more
REPEAT AD LIB. AND FADE
GM7 C7 F DM7 GM7 C7 F DM7
sail-ing.) No more sail - ing. (No more sail-ing.) So long sail-ing. (No more

BIRD FEATHERS

BY CHARLIE PARKER

MEDIUM-UP SWING
A
Bb6
Bb7(#5)
Eb6
3
Ab7
3
BbMAJ7
G7
CM7
TO CODA
F9
DM7
C#DIM7
CM7
F7(#9 #5)
B
SOLOS:
Bb7
Eb7
Bb7
DM7
G7
AFTER LAST SOLO D.S. AL CODA
CM7
F7
Bb7
CM7
F7
CODA
Bb
G13
CM7
F7(#9)
Bb6

BIRD'S NEST

FAST BE-BOP

BY CHARLIE PARKER

A
Bb6/9 GM7 CM7 F7 Bb6/9 GM7 CM7 F7
Bb6/9 Bb7 Eb7 EDIM7 Bb6/9 GM7 CM7 F7
Bb6/9 GM7 CM7 F7 Bb6/9 GM7 CM7 F7
Bb6/9 Bb7 Eb7 EDIM Bb6/9
B
Eb7 EDIM7 Bb6/9 Bb7
Eb7 DM7(b5) G7(b9) C7 F7
C
Bb6/9 GM7 CM7 F7 Bb6/9 GM7 CM7 F7
Bb6/9 Bb7 Eb7 EDIM Bb6/9 (GM7 CM7 F7)

BLACK NILE

BY WAYNE SHORTER

MEDIUM-UP SWING

INTRO: FM9 G♭MAJ7 E♭M7 FM7 DM7
B♭13 E♭MAJ9 EM9(♭5) A7(♯9 ♯5) A DM6
(87)
E♭9 DM6 CM7 F7(♭9 ♯5) B♭MAJ7
A7(♯5) DM6 E♭9 DM6 E♭9
(87)
DM6 CM7 F7(♭9 ♯5) B♭MAJ7 GM7 C9SUS A7(♯9 ♯5)
B
A♭13 GM11 C13 FM7 B♭7 E♭MAJ7
C
GM11 C13 FM7 B♭7 E♭MAJ7 A7(♯9 ♯5) DM6
(87)
E♭9 DM6 CM7 F7(♭9 ♯5) B♭MAJ7 A7(♯5)
1
DM6 E♭9
2
DM6 A7(♯5) DM6 A7(♯5) DM6

BLUE AND SENTIMENTAL

WORDS & MUSIC BY COUNT BASIE, JERRY LIVINGSTON AND MACK DAVID

BLACKBERRY WINTER

MODERATELY SLOW

WORDS AND MUSIC BY
ALEC WILDER AND LOONIS McGLOHON

B
(Cm7/Eb)
EbMaj7 F/Eb Dm7 Gm7
I'll nev - er get o - ver los - ing you, but I've had to
Cm7 F7 (Bm7(b5) E7(b9)) BbMaj7 Am Am(Maj7)/G#
learn that life goes on. And the mem - o - ries grow dim
Am7/G Am6/F# Bm7(b5) E7(b9)
like a half - for - got - ten song, 'til a black - ber - ry win - ter re -
Am7 (D7(#5)) Ab13 Gm7 C7(b9)
minds me you are gone. And
C
FMaj7 Am7
I get so lone - ly
Dm7 Gm7 C9sus FMaj7 (Bb9) Gm7
most of all in spring time. I wish I could en - joy the first of
Am7 BbMaj7 Am7 Dm7 Gm7 C7
May, but I know it means that black - ber - ry win - ter is not too far a -
1
F6 Gm7 C7
way.
2
F6 BbMaj7 FMaj7
way.

Dizzy Gillespie
Courtesy of Star File, Inc.

BLUE 'N BOOGIE

MEDIUM-UP SWING

MUSIC BY JOHN "DIZZY" GILLESPIE

BLUE RONDO A LA TURK

MEDIUM-UP
MUSIC BY DAVE BRUBECK
A
FMAJ7 F7 F6 F+ F F+ F6 F7 FMAJ7 F7 F6 F+
F F+ F6 AM7 A6 F/A AM7 ADIM AM F/A D7/A
AM7 A6 F/A AM7 ADIM AM DM7/A FMAJ7 F7 F6 F+
F F+ F6 F7 FMAJ7 F7 F6 F+ F F+ F6
B
AM DM6/A AM7 BDIM7/A AM7 DM6/A AM B7 AM DM6/A AM7 BDIM7/A
AM7 D7/A DM7/A FMAJ7 F7 F6 F+ F F+ F6 F7
FMAJ7 F7 F6 F+ F F+ F6
C
AM7 DM6/A AM7 DM6/A

Am7 Dm6/A A Dm7
Fmaj7 F7 F6 F+
F F+ F6 F7 Fmaj7 F7 F6 F+ F F+ F6
D
A Am G/A Dm/A Am Am6 Dm/A Am A Dm A
A Am D/A Dm6/A Am F
G Gm F/G G G7 C/G Cm/G G F
To Coda
Em Dm7 C Am7 F Em Dm7 Em7 A G/A A G/A
A G/A A Dm7 F A G/A F/A

E
EASY BLUES ♩.= ♩
F7 Bb7 FMAJ7 F7 F6 F+ F F+ F6 F7
Bb7 FMAJ7 F7 F6 F+ F F+ F6 F7
GM7 C7 FMAJ7 F7 F6 F+ F F+ F6 F7
F
BLUES
SOLOS
F7 Bb7 F7 Bb7
AFTER LAST SOLO D.S. AL CODA
F7 D7 GM7 C7 F7 D7 GM7 C7
CODA
A G/A A G/A A G/A
A DM7 F
A/E EM7 F/E EM7 A
RIT.

BLUES FOR ALICE

MEDIUM-UP SWING

BY CHARLIE PARKER

*BLUE TRAIN

BY JOHN COLTRANE

* FROM THE ORIGINAL JOHN COLTRANE RECORDING, "BLUE TRAIN".

BLUE TRAIN

* (ALTERNATE VERSION)

BY JOHN COLTRANE

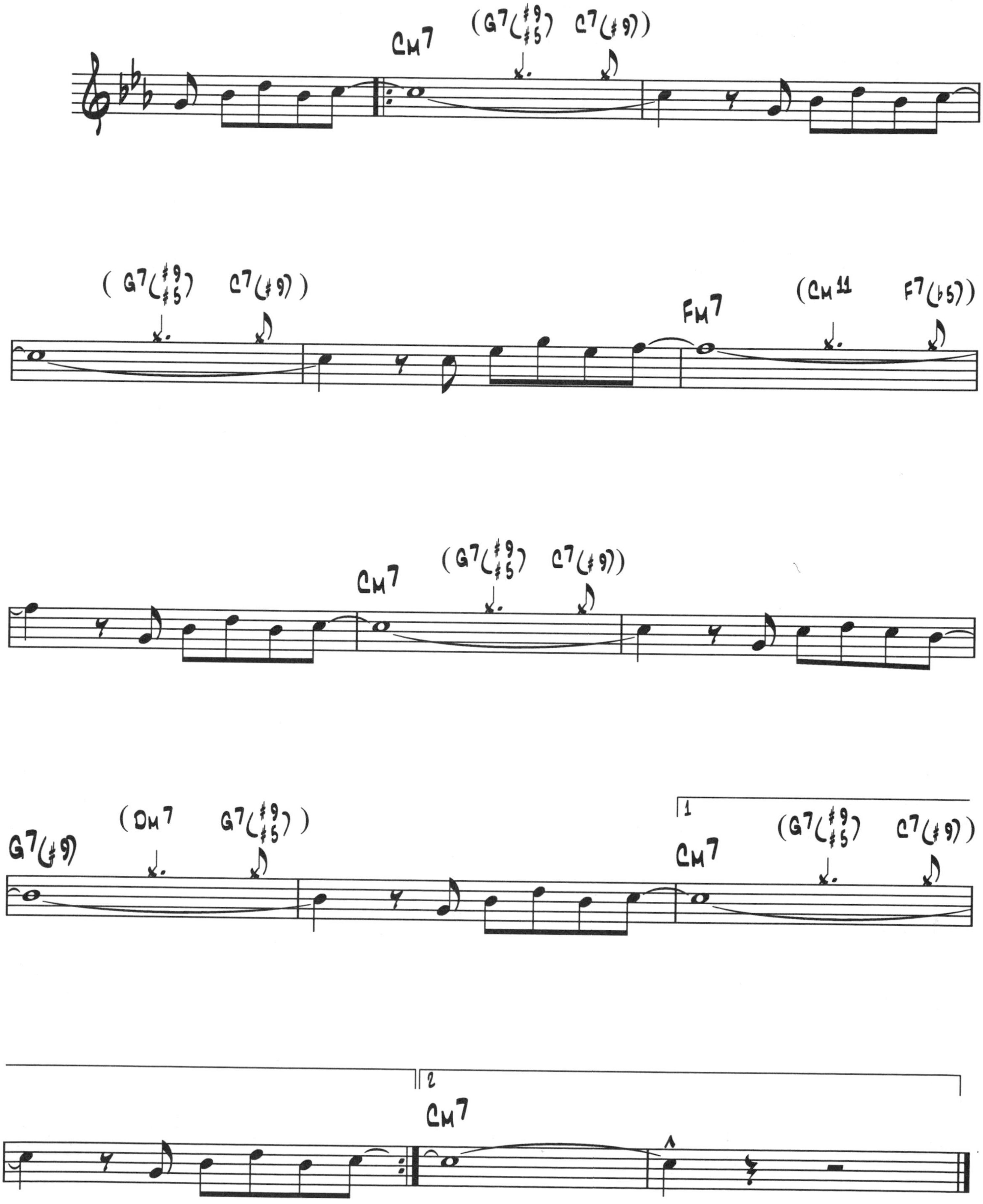

* THIS ARRANGEMENT REPRESENTS THE MOST COMMONLY PERFORMED VERSION.

BLUESETTE

WORDS BY NORMAN GIMBEL
MUSIC BY JEAN THIELEMANS

MEDIUM JAZZ WALTZ

F9 DM7 (G7(b9)) Db7 CM7 (F7(#9 #5)) F7
oo, blues - ette.
C
BbMAJ7 AM7(b5) D7(b9) GM7
Pret-ty lit-tle blue-ette must-n't be a mourn-er. Have you heard the
C7 FM7 Bb7 EbMAJ7
news yet? Love is 'round the cor - ner. Love wrapped in
(Eb6) EbM7 Ab7 DbMAJ7
rain - bows and tied with pink rib - bons to make your next Spring-time your
DbM7 Gb7 CbMAJ7 CM7
gold wed - ding ring time. So dry your eyes. Don't-cha pout, don't-cha
F7 DM7 (G7(b9)) Db7 CM7 (F7(#9 #5)) F7 D.C. AL CODA
fret, good-y good times are com - ing, blues - ette.
CODA
CbMAJ7 CM7 F7 DM7
One luck - y day love - ly love will come your way.
G7(#5) G7 CM11 F7SUS
That mag - ic day may
REPEAT AD LIB. AND FADE
Bb7(#9) Cb7(#9) Bb7(#9) Cb7(#9)
just be to - day.

BODY AND SOUL

WORDS BY EDWARD HEYMAN, ROBERT SOUR AND FRANK EYTON
MUSIC BY JOHNNY GREEN

BALLAD

BONGO BEEP

MEDIUM SWINGING LATIN

BY CHARLIE PARKER

BONGO BOP

BY CHARLIE PARKER

MEDIUM BLUES

B CHORD CHANGES FOR SOLOS:

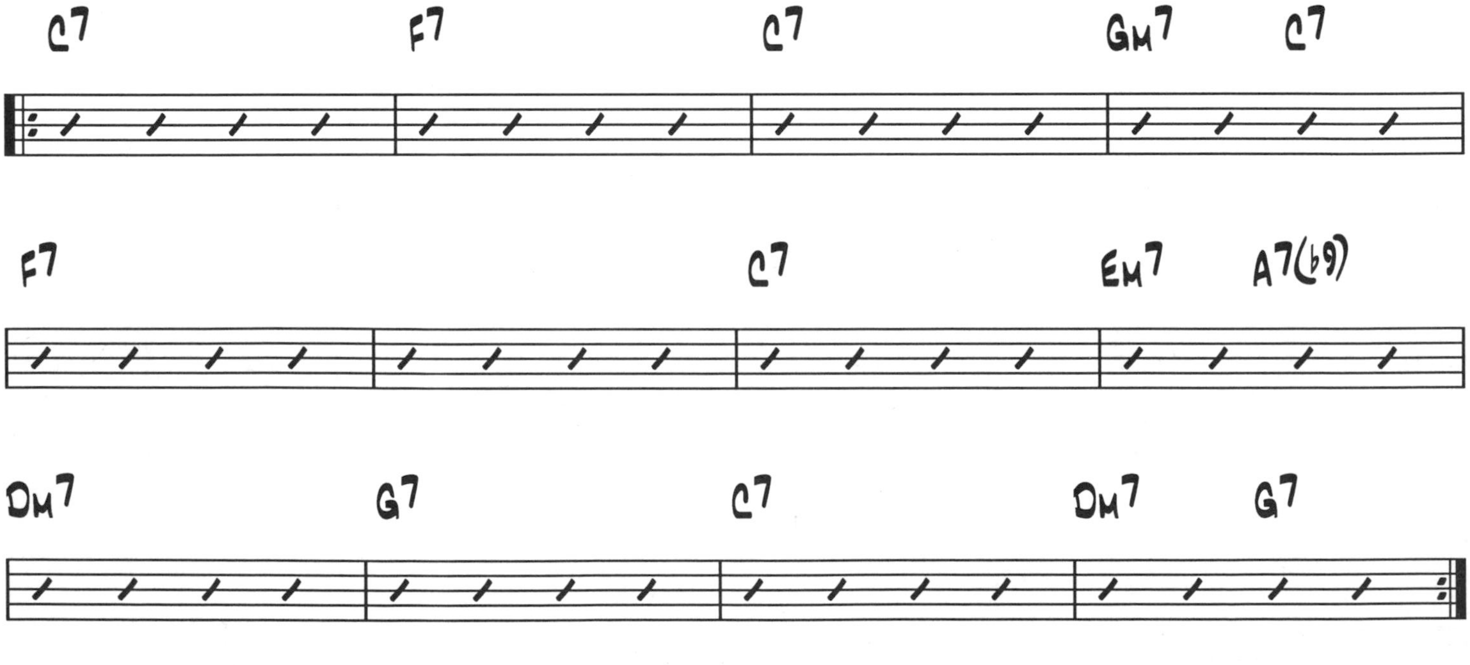

BETWEEN THE DEVIL AND THE DEEP BLUE SEA

Words by TED KOEHLER
Music by HAROLD ARLEN

MEDIUM

THE BOULEVARD OF BROKEN DREAMS

WORDS BY AL DUBIN
MUSIC BY HARRY WARREN

B
Am7(b5)
D7(b9)
Gm
Gm(maj7)
find me, always walk-ing up and down;
Gm7
C7
Gm
Gm(maj7)
Gm7
C7
F
Fmaj7
F6
but I left my soul be-hind me,
C13
in an old ca-the-dral town;
C
A7
Dm
Gm
Dm
the joy that you find here you bor-row, you can-not keep it long it
Em7(b5)
Bb13
A7
seems. But gig-o-lo and gig-o-lette,
Em7(b5)
A7
still sing a song and dance a-long the bou-le-vard of bro-ken
1
Dm
Gm
Dm
2
Dm
Gm
Dm
dreams. I walk a-long the street of dreams.

BUT BEAUTIFUL

SLOW/MED.

WORDS BY JOHNNY BURKE
MUSIC BY JIMMY VAN HEUSEN

CANTALOUPE ISLAND

BY HERBIE HANCOCK

BYE BYE BLACKBIRD

WORDS BY MORT DIXON
MUSIC BY RAY HENDERSON

Gm7 C7 D7(b9) Gm7
black - bird. Where some - bod - y
D7(#5) Gm7 C7
waits for me, sug - ar's sweet, so is she.
Gm7 Bbmaj7/C (C13(b9)) F Gm7 C7
Bye bye black - bird,
B
F7 Am7(b5) D7(b9)
No one here can love and un - der - stand me.
Gm7 Gm7(b5) C7
Oh, what hard luck sto - ries they all hand me.
C
F Am7(b5)
Make my bed and light the light, I'll ar - rive
D7(b9) Gm7 C7
late to - night. Black - bird, bye
1
F Gm7 C7
bye.
(OPTIONAL D.C.)
2
F Eb9 F
bye.

CARAVAN

UP-TEMPO LATIN

WORDS & MUSIC BY DUKE ELLINGTON,
IRVING MILLS AND JUAN TIZOL

C
C7(♭9)
(D♭7
C7(♭9)
D♭7)
you_ be - side me, here be - neath the
(C7(♭9)
D♭7
C7(♭9)
D♭7)
blue._ My dream of love is com - ing
(C7(♭9)
D♭7
C7(♭9))
true_ with - in our des - ert car - a -
Fm6
van._
ALTERNATE INSTRUMENTAL MELODY AT LETTER B :
SWING
F9
F13
B♭9
E♭7
E♭9
A♭6
C7

Cast Your Fate to the Wind
(Instrumental Version)

Gentle Latin

By Vince Guaraldi

CAST YOUR FATE TO THE WIND
(OPTIONAL VOCAL VERSION)

GENTLE LATIN

BY VINCE GUARALDI AND CAREL WERBER

A
C/F F C/F Bb/F
1. A month of nights, a year of days, Oc - to - bers drift - ing in - to
shift your course a - long the breeze, won't sail up - wind on mem - o -
C/F F
TO CODA
Mays. You set your sail when the tide comes in and you just
ries. The emp - ty sky is your best friend and you just
Bb C7 F Bb C Bb F Bb C Bb C Bb
1,3
2
cast your fate to the wind.
2. You
B
F C7 F Bb C7 F Bb C7
That time has such a way of chang-ing a man through - out the years. And
F Bb C7 F Bb C7 F
now you're re - ar - rang - ing your life thru all your tears a - lone,
Bb C7 F Bb C7 F
D.S. AL CODA
(USE REPEAT)
a - lone.
3. There
CODA
Bb C7 F
cast your fate to the wind.

Verse 3
There never was, there couldn't be
A place in time for men to be,
Who'd drink the dark and laugh at day
And let their wildest dreams blow away.

Verse 4
So now you're old, you're wise, you're smart,
You're just a man with half a heart.
You wonder how it might have been
Had you not cast your fate to the wind.

CENTRAL PARK WEST

MEDIUM BALLAD

BY JOHN COLTRANE

A CHILD IS BORN

MEDIUM JAZZ WALTZ

BY THAD JONES

A
BbMAJ7 EbM6/Bb BbMAJ7 EbM6/Bb BbMAJ7
Now (born.) out of the night, new as the dawn,
EbM6/Bb Bb AM7(b5) D7(b9) GM7 D7(b9)
in - to the light, this child, in - no - cent
GM7 D7(b9) GM7 C7 EbMAJ7/F F7
child, soft as a fawn, this child is born. One small
B
BbMAJ7 EbM6/Bb BbMAJ7 EbM6/Bb BbMAJ7
heart, one pair of eyes, one work of art
D7(#9 #5) EbMAJ9 Ab9 (Ab9/Gb) CM7(b5) BbMAJ7/F EbM6/Gb
here in my arms. Here he lies, trust - ing and
GM7 C7 EbMAJ7/F 1 F7 2 F7
warm, bless - ed this morn a child is child is
BbMAJ7 EbM6/Bb BbMAJ7 EbM6/Bb BbMAJ7
born.

* CHAMELEON

BY HERBIE HANCOCK

* AS RECORDED BY HERBIE HANCOCK ON THE ORIGINAL RECORDING, "HEADHUNTERS".

C
OPTIONAL SOLO SECTIONS
BbM7
Eb7
BbM7
Eb7
BASS RIFF CONTINUES
N.C.
PLAY 4 TIMES
Db
BbM
D
BbM9
AbM9/Db
BbM9
AbM9/Db
E
BM7
C/D
Bb/C
E(9)/G#
BbM11
BM9
C/D
1,2
AbM9/Db
BbM9
AbM9/Db
BbM9
AbM9/Db
3
N.C.
Db
BM

CHEGA DE SAUDADE
(No More Blues)

MEDIUM BOSSA

ORIGINAL TEXT BY VINICIUS DE MORAES
MUSIC BY ANTONIO CARLOS JOBIM
ENGLISH LYRIC BY JON HENDRICKS AND JESSIE CAVANAUGH

C
DMAJ7 B7(#5)/D# EM7
Ev' - ry day while I am far a - way my thoughts turn home-
A9SUS A7 DDIM7 DMAJ7
ward, for-ev - er home - ward. I trav-
F#M7 FDIM7 EM7
elled 'round the world in search of hap - pi - ness, but all my hap-
E9 GM6 A7(b9)
pi - ness I found was in my home - town.
D
DMAJ7 BM7 E7
No more blues, I'm goin' back home, no, no
F#7 BM7 BbM7 AM7 (Ab7) D7
more dues. I'm through with all my wan - drin' now. I'll set-
GMAJ7 GM7 F#M7 B13 B7(#5)
tle down and live my life and build a home and find a wife. When we
E9 A13 F#M7 B7(#5)
set - tle down, there'll be no more blues, noth-in' but hap - pi - ness. When we
E9 A9SUS D6/9 A7(#5) D6/9
set - tle down there'll be no more blues.
1
2

CHRISTMAS TIME IS HERE

WORDS & MUSIC BY
LEE MENDELSON AND VINCE GUARALDI

SLOWLY

COME SUNDAY

GOSPEL BALLAD

BY DUKE ELLINGTON

A
F7
Eb9(#11)
F7
(Gb7)
(D7(b9 #5)) G9
Lord, dear Lord a - bove: God al - might - y; God of love,
Cm9
F9
(GbMAJ7 BMAJ7 E7(b5))
Bb Eb6/Bb Bbdim7 Bb6
please look down and see my peo - ple through.
B
D7 Eb7 D7 Gm7 C9-13
I be - lieve that God put sun and moon up in the sky;
Heav - en is a good - ness time. A bright - er light on high.
I be - lieve God is now, was then and al - ways will be.
F7 Cm7 F7 Ab13 G7(#5) C9 F7(#5)
I don't mind the gray skies, 'cause they're just clouds pass - ing by.
(spoken): Do unto others as you would have them do to you. And have a bright - er by and by.
With God's bless - ing we can make it through e - ter - ni - ty.
C
F7
Eb9(#11)
F7
(Gb7)
D7(b9 #5)
G9
Lord, dear Lord a - bove: God al - might - y; God of love,
Cm9
F9
Bb Eb6/Bb
1,2
Bbdim7 Bb6
3
Bbdim7 Bb6
please look down and see my peo - ple through.

COME BACK TO ME

LYRIC BY ALAN JAY LERNER
MUSIC BY BURTON LANE

A
LIVELY
GM7 C7SUS C7 GM7 C7SUS C7
Hear your voice, where you are! Take a train; steal a car; hop a
hide, hear me call! Must I fight ci - ty hall? Here and
FMAJ7 F6 FMAJ7 F6 FMAJ7
freight; grab a star; come back to me! Catch a
now, damn it all, come back to me! What on
GM7 C7SUS C7 GM7 C7SUS C7
plane; catch a breeze; on your hands, on your knees; swim or
earth must I do, scream and yell till I'm blue? Curse your
FMAJ7 F6 FMAJ7 F6 FMAJ7
fly, on - ly please, come back to me! On a
soul when will you come back to me? Have you
B
AM7 F/A D/A E7 AM7 BM7(♭5) E7
mule, in a jet, with your hair in a net, with a tow'l wring-ing wet, I don't
gone to the moon or the cor - ner sa-loon and to rack and to "roon"? Mad-moi -
CMAJ7 AM/C D9 D9(♯5) GM7 C7SUS C7
care, this is where you should be. From the
selle, where in hell can you be? In a

C
GM7 C7SUS C7 AM7(b5) D7
hills, from the shore, ride the wind to my door. Turn the
crate! In a trunk! On a horse! On a drunk! In a
G7 (BbM7) GM7(b5) FMAJ7 BM7(b5)
high - way to dust, break the law if you must; move the
Rolls or a van, wrapped in mink or Sa - ran; an - y
F/C Ab7 GM7 C7 F6/9
world on - ly just come back to me! Come
way that you can, come back to me! Come
Bb7 1 F6/9
back to me! Come back to me!
back to me! Come
AM7(b5) D7(b9) 2 F6/9
Blast your back to me!
OFTEN PERFORMED AS FAST DOUBLE TIME:
GM7 C7SUS C7
Hear your voice, where you are! Take a
GM7 C7SUS C7 ETC.
train; steal a car; hop a

CONFIRMATION

UP-TEMPO BE-BOP

BY CHARLIE PARKER

A
F
EM7(b5)
A7
DM
CM7
F7(#5)
FM7
Bb7
AM7(b5)
D7
G7
C7(b9)
F
EM7(b5)
A7
DM
CM7
F7
FM7
Bb7
AM7(b5)
D7
GM7
C7
B
F
CM
CM(MAJ7)
CM7
F7ALT
BbMAJ7
EbM7
Ab7
DbMAJ7
C
GM7
C7ALT
F
EM7(b5)
A7
DM
CM7
F7(#5)
FM7
Bb7
AM7(b5)
D7
GM7
C7
F

COOL BLUES

BY CHARLIE PARKER

MEDIUM BLUES

A
C7
C7(#11)
F7
C7(#11)
Dm7
G7
C7(#11)
B
SOLOS:
C7
F7
C7
Dm7
G7
C7
Dm7
G7

COTTON TAIL

Music by DUKE ELLINGTON
Words by JON HENDRICKS

* COUNTDOWN

FAST

BY JOHN COLTRANE

* AS PLAYED BY JOHN COLTRANE ON THE RECORDING, "GIANT STEPS"

** CUE NOTE NOT PLAYED BY COLTRANE ON ORIGINAL RECORDING

CRYSTAL SILENCE

BALLAD

BY CHICK COREA AND NEVILLE POTTER

CUTE

MEDIUM SWING

Music by NEAL HEFTI

A
(F6) (Eb9)
Dm7 Em7 A7(b9 #5) Dm7 G9 C6 A7 A7(b9)
(DRUM FILL)
(F6) (Eb9)
Dm7 Em7 A7(b9 #5) Dm9 G9 Gm7 C7 Gm7 C9
(DR. FILL)
Fmaj7 Em7 Dm7 Fm6 Cmaj7 F9 E7 Am7
(DR. FILL)
(DR. FILL)
(Em7) (F#m11 B9)
Am6 C/G F#m7(b5) B9 Emaj7 Em7(b5) A7(b9)
(DR. FILL)
B
(F6) (Eb9)
Dm7 Em7 A7(b9 #5) Dm7 G9 C6 A7 A7(b9)
(DR. FILL)
(F6) (Eb9)
Dm7 Em7 A7(b9 #5) Dm9 G9 Gm7 C7 Gm7 C9
(DR. FILL)
Fmaj7 Em7 Dm7 Fm6 Cmaj7 F9 E7 Am7
(DR. FILL)
(DR. FILL)
(F6) (Eb7(#11))
Dm7 Em7 A7(#5) Dm7 G7(b9) C6/9
1
Em7(b5) A7(#5)
2
Db9 C9
(DR. FILL)

A DAY IN THE LIFE OF A FOOL

WORDS BY CARL SIGMAN
MUSIC BY LUIZ BONFA

DEACON BLUES

WORDS AND MUSIC BY
WALTER BECKER AND DONALD FAGEN

MODERATELY

8
G6 F6 G/A F6
You call me a fool, you say it's a cra - zy scheme.
I crawl like a vi - per through these sub - ur - ban streets,
This is the night of the ex - pand - ing man.
G6 F6 G/A A9
This one's for real I al - read - y bought the dream.
love to these wom - en, lan - guid and bit - ter sweet.
I take one last drag as I ap - proach the stand.
FMAJ7 E7(b9)
So use - less to ask me why
I'll rise when the sun goes down,
I cried when I wrote this song,
AM7 GM7 C9 FMAJ7
throw a kiss and say good - bye. I'll make it this
cov - er ev - 'ry game in town. A world of my
sue me if I play too long. This broth - er is
EM7(#5) D9 F/G
time, I'm read - y to cross that fine line.
own. I'll make it my home, sweet home.
free. I'll be what I want to be.
C CHORUS:
AM7 EM7 DM7 CMAJ7
Learn to work the sax - o - phone. I'll play just what I feel.
BbMAJ7 AM7 G6 F#7(b5) FMAJ7 EM7(#5)
Drink Scotch whis - key all night long and die
FMAJ7 AM7 EM7
be - hind the wheel. They got a name for the win - ners in the world,

DM7
CMAJ7
BbMAJ7
I want a name when I lose. They call Al - a - bam - a the
AM7
G6
F#7(b5)
FMAJ7
EM7(#5)
FMAJ7
Crim - son Tide, call me Dea - con Blues.
TO CODA
AM7
EM7
DMAJ7
C#M7(#5)
CMAJ7
BM7(#5)
EbMAJ7
E7(#9)
BbM6
BM7(#5)
CMAJ7
EM7
A13
D7(#9)
G13
B7(#9)
EM7
A9
FMAJ7
F#7(b5)
GMAJ7
B7(#5)
CMAJ7
BM7(#5)
BbMAJ7
AM7(#5)
D.S. AL CODA
DMAJ7
DbM7(#5)
CMAJ7
BM7(#5)
EbMAJ9
E7(#9)
CODA
FMAJ7
EM7(#5)
RIT.
FMAJ7
AM7
call me Dea - con Blues.

DESAFINADO

MEDIUM BOSSA

WORDS BY JON HENDRICKS & JESSIE CAVANAUGH
MUSIC BY ANTONIO CARLOS JOBIM

(F♯m7(♭5)) (B♭7(♯11))
Amaj7 Am7 Bm7 E7
Now the song is dif - f'rent and the words don't e - ven rhyme; 'cause you
Cmaj7 C♯dim7 Dm7 G7
for - got the mel - o - dy our hearts would al - ways croon, and so what
Gm7 E♭m6 G7 C7(♭9)
good's a heart that's slight - ly out of tune?
C
Fmaj7 G7(♭5)
Tune your heart to mine the way it used to be,
Gm7 C7 Am7(♭5)
join with me in har - mo - ny and sing a song of lov -
(Gm7) (Fmaj7)
D7(♭9) B♭maj7 B♭m6 Am7
ing, we're bound to get in tune a - gain be - fore too long,
(Dm7) (E♭9)
A♭dim7 G7 G♭maj7
there'll be no de - sa - fi - na - do when your heart be - longs to me com - plete -
G7 Gm7 C7
ly, then you won't be slight - ly out of tune, you'll sing a - long
1 F6 C7(♯9) C7(♭9)
with me.
2 F6/9
with me.

DEXTERITY

BE-BOP

BY CHARLIE PARKER

A
Bb CM7 F7(b9)
Bb G7 CM7 F7 Bb Bb7
Eb Ab7 1 DM7 Db7 CM7 F7
2 CM7 F7ALT Bb B AM7 D7
AM7 D7 DM7 G7
GM7 C7 CM7
C
F7 Bb CM7 F7(b9)
Bb G7 CM7 F7 Bb Bb7
Eb Ab7 CM7 F7ALT Bb

DO NOTHIN' TILL YOU HEAR FROM ME

SLOW / MED

MUSIC BY DUKE ELLINGTON
LYRIC BY BOB RUSSELL

DIZZY ATMOSPHERE

FAST SWING

BY JOHN "DIZZY" GILLESPIE

Bbm7
Eb7(b9)
Ab6
Db6
B
Ab6
Eb9
D9
D13
Db9
Db13
C13
B13
Bb13
A13
C
Ab6
Fm7
Bbm7
Eb7(b9)
Ab6
Fm7
Bbm7
Eb7(b9)
Ab6
Fm7
Bbm7
Eb7(b9)
Ab6
Db6
1
Ab6
Bbm6
2
Ab6

DO IT AGAIN

WORDS AND MUSIC BY WALTER BECKER AND DONALD FAGEN

man is - n't hang - in' and they put
— you know she's smil - in' you'll be on
— of milk and hon - ey you must put
you on the street.
your knees to - mor - row.
them on the ta - ble.
Yeah, you go
8
Chorus:
Cm7 Dm7 Ebmaj7 Dm7 Gm7
back Jack, do it a - gain, wheel turn - ing round
Cm7 Dm7 Ebmaj7 Dm7
and round. You go back Jack, do it a - gain.
Gm7
1
2
3
2. When you know
3. Now you swear
Gm7
Repeat ad lib. and fade

DOLPHIN DANCE

BY HERBIE HANCOCK

MEDIUM SWING
EbMAJ7 Bbm9/Eb EbMAJ7 Dm7(b5) G7
A
Cm7 Ab9(#11) Cm7 Am7 D7 GMAJ7
Abm7 (Db7) Fm11 (Bb7) Cm7 (Cm7/Bb)
B
Am11 D13 GMAJ7 G9SUS A/G EbMAJ7(b5)/G
F9SUS F13(b9) F9SUS Em9 A13 Eb9(#11)
Am7 D13 Bm7 E13 Dm7 C#m11
F#13 Bm9/E Am9/E Bm9/E Am9/E Bbm9/Eb
(LAST TIME)
Bb13(b9)/Eb C7(#9)/Eb G7(#9 #5)
REPEAT FOR SOLOS
Bm9/E Am9/E
REPEAT AD LIB. AND FADE

DON'T EXPLAIN

BALLAD

WORDS BY ARTHUR HERZOG, JR.
MUSIC BY BILLIE HOLIDAY

DON'T BLAME ME

MUSIC BY JIMMY McHUGH
LYRIC BY DOROTHY FIELDS

FREELY
VERSE:

DM7 G7(#5) CMAJ7 DM11 G13 CMAJ7 EM7(b5) A7(#5) A7
Don't blame me. Can't you see, when
(AM7)
DM7(b5) G13 CMAJ9 DM7(b5) G13
you do the things you do, if I can't con - ceal the
EM7(b5) A7(#5) A7 DM7 G13 C C7
way that I'm feel - ing, don't blame me.
B
F E7 AM11 E7(#5) AM
I can't help it if that dog - goned moon a - bove
(Eb13 D7 DM7/G DM7(b5))
D7 D7 G9 Ab13 G13
makes me need some - one like you to love.
C
CMAJ7 EM7(b5) A7(#5) A7 DM7(b5) G13
Blame your kiss, as sweet as a kiss can
(AM7)
CMAJ7 DM7(b5) G13 EM7(b5) A7(#5) A7
be. And blame all your charms that melt in my arms but
1 (OPTIONAL D.C.) 2
DM7 G13 C DM11 G13 C
don't blame me. me.

DON'T GET AROUND MUCH ANYMORE

MUSIC BY DUKE ELLINGTON
LYRIC BY BOB RUSSELL

DONNA LEE

FAST SWING

BY CHARLIE PARKER

A
(Cm7 F7)
Ab F7 Bb7
Bbm7 Eb7 Ab Ebm7 Ab7
(D7)
(Dbm7)
Db Gb7 Ab F7
Bb7 Bbm7 Eb7
B
Ab F7 Bb7
(Gm7(b5) C7)
C7 Fm C7(#9)
(Abdim7)
Fm C7 Fm Bbdim7
(Ab)
Cm7 F7 Bbm7 Eb7
1
Ab Bbm7 Eb7
2
Ab

DRIFTING ON A REED

BY CHARLIE PARKER

MEDIUM BLUES

DUKE'S PLACE
(A/K/A C JAM BLUES)

MUSIC BY DUKE ELLINGTON
LYRICS BY RUTH ROBERTS, BILL KATZ
AND ROBERT THIELE

THE DUKE

MEDIUM SWING

MUSIC BY DAVE BRUBECK

A
CMAJ7 FMAJ7 /F# EM/G AM7 B7 EM7 AM7
DM9 FM7 Bb7 EbMAJ7 DbMAJ7 CM7 BM7
BbM7 Eb7 AbMAJ7 D7 G7 D7 Db7(b9) CMAJ7 Gb7
B
FMAJ7 E9 D7 CMAJ7 BbM7 AbMAJ7 G7(b9) FM7
DM7(b5) G7 CM7 CM7(b5) F7(#9) BbM7 Ab/C BbM7 Ab6 GM7(b5)

C
Fm9 Eb9sus Db13(#11) Cmaj7 Fmaj7 /F# Em/G Am7 B7
3
Em7 Am7 Dm9 Fm7 Bb7 Ebmaj7 Dbmaj7
To Coda
D.S. al Coda
Cm7 Bm7 Bbm7 Eb7 Abmaj7 D7 Db7(b5) Cmaj7
Coda
D7 G7 Cmaj7 Em7/G Cmaj7/E Fm(maj7)/C Fm6/Ab
Em/G Dm/F C/E Bdim/D Am/C G#dim/B Am7 Em7/B Cmaj7/G
Am7/E Fm6 Adim7 C6/G C6/E Dm7 F6 Fmaj7/C G13(b9)/B C6

EARLY AUTUMN

MEDIUM

WORDS BY JOHNNY MERCER
MUSIC BY RALPH BURNS AND WOODY HERMAN

B
CMAJ7 C6 CMAJ7 C6 DM7 G7 CMAJ7 Ebdim7
lone - ly. That spring of ours that start - ed so A - pril heart - ed
DM7 G7 CMAJ7 C6 CM7 F7
seemed made for just a boy and girl. I nev - er dreamed, did you, an - y
BbMAJ7 Eb7 DMAJ7 C#7 C9 B7(#9) Bb7 AMAJ7 Ab13(b9) G9
fall could come in view so ear - ly, ear - ly?
C
CMAJ7 B7 BbMAJ7
Dar - ling, if you care please let me know, I'll meet you an - y - where.
A7 AbMAJ7 G7 G7(b9 b5)
I miss you so, let's nev - er have to share an - oth - er ear - ly
1 2
C6/9 AM7 DM7 G7 CMAJ7 G7(b9) C6/9
au - tumn. When an ear - ly au - tumn.

EASY TO LOVE

WORDS & MUSIC BY COLE PORTER

FREELY
VERSE:
BbMAJ7 GM BbMAJ7 GM CM7
I know too well that I'm just wast-ing pre-cious time in think-ing such a
F13 BbMAJ7 CM7 F7SUS F7 BbMAJ7 F7(b9) Bb
thing could be, that you could ev-er care for me. I'm sure you hate to hear that I a -
GM E7(b5) DMAJ7 GMAJ7 EM7 A13 D Eb7
dore you, dear, but grant me, just the same, I'm not en - tire - ly to blame, for:
A
SLOWLY
CHORUS:
AM7 DM7 E7(b9) AM7 D7 GMAJ7 CMAJ7
You'd be so eas - y to love, so eas - y to i - do - lize, all
G Bb7 AM7 D9 GMAJ7 BM7 E7(b9)
oth - ers a - bove, so worth the yearn-ing for,
AM7 D7(b9) D9 BM7 BbDIM7
so swell to keep ev - 'ry home fire burn - ing for.
B
AM7 DM7 E7(b9) AM7 D7 GMAJ7 CMAJ7
We'd be so grand at the game, so care - free to - geth - er, that it
BM7 E7SUS E7(b9) AM11 CM7 F9 GMAJ7 C7(#11) BM7 BbDIM7
does seem a shame, that you can't see your fu - ture with me. 'Cause you'd be
AM7 D13(b9) 1 G BM7 E7(b9) 2 G
oh, so eas - y to love! love!

EMILY

MODERATELY SLOW WALTZ
OR JAZZ WALTZ

MUSIC BY JOHNNY MANDEL
LYRIC BY JOHNNY MERCER

Em - i - ly, Em - i - ly, Em - i - ly has the mur - mer-ing
sound of May. All sil - ver bells, cor - al shells, car - ou - sels,
and the laugh - ter of chil - dren at play say
Em - i - ly, Em - i - ly, Em - i - ly. And we fade to a
mar - ve - lous view, two lov - ers a - lone and
out of sight see - ing im - ag - es in the fire - light.
As my eyes vis - ual - ize a fam - i - ly, they see
dream - i - ly, Em - i - ly too. too.

EMBRACEABLE YOU

Music and Lyrics by
GEORGE GERSHWIN and IRA GERSHWIN

(F♯m7 B7(♭9))
Am Am7(♭5) D7 G6/9 D9sus G6/9
Em - brace me, you ir - re - place - a - ble you.
Em Em7/D C♯m7(♭5) F♯7 Bm Bm(maj7) Bm7 E9
Just one look at you, my heart grew tip - sy in me;
D/A D♯dim7 Em7 A9 D13 Am7 D7
You and you a - lone bring out the gyp - sy in me!
B
(B♭dim7 Am7 D7 E7)
G6 Gdim7 D7 C(9)/E Dm7(♭5)/F D7/F♯
I love all the man - y charms a - bout you;
Am Am7(♭5) D7 Gmaj7 Dm7 G7(♯5)
a - bove all I want my arms a - bout you.
(Em/D)
Cmaj7 F♯m7(♭5) B7 Em Em(maj7)
Don't be a naugh - ty ba - by, come to pa - pa, come to
(C♯m7(♭5) Cm6 Bm7 E7(♭9))
Em7 A9/C♯ G/D Am7(♭5) D7(♭9)
pa - pa, do! My sweet em - brace - a - ble
1 G6/9 Am7 D7
you!
2 G6/9
you!

DAYS OF WINE AND ROSES

LYRIC BY JOHNNY MERCER
MUSIC BY HENRY MANCINI

EPISTROPHY

BY THELONIUS MONK
AND CLARKE KENNY

MEDIUM SWING

ESP

BY WAYNE SHORTER

FAST SWING
E7ALT
FMAJ7
E7ALT
EbMAJ7
D7ALT
(Eb7)
EbMAJ7
E7ALT
FMAJ7
EbMAJ7
1
DM9
G7
GM7
(C7ALT)
GbMAJ9
2
Db9(#11)
GM7
3
DbM7
Gb7
FMAJ7

FALL

MEDIUM BALLAD (SWING FEEL)

BY WAYNE SHORTER
(AS PLAYED BY MILES DAVIS)

EUROPA
(EARTH'S CRY HEAVEN'S SMILE)

BY CARLOS SANTANA AND TOM COSTER

F7
B♭MAJ7
E♭MAJ7
AM7(♭5)
D7(♭9)
GM
3
3
3
CM7
F7
B♭MAJ7
E♭MAJ7
AM7(♭5)
D7(♭9)
1
TO NEXT STRAIN
2,3 ETC.
REPEAT AD LIB. AND FADE
GM
3
C
CM7
F7
B♭MAJ7
E♭MAJ7
AM7(♭5)
D7(♭9)
GMAJ7
D.S. 𝄋

EVERYTIME WE SAY GOODBYE

WORDS & MUSIC BY COLE PORTER

8
EbMAJ7 CM7 FM7 Bb13 EbMAJ7 CM7
When you're near___ there's such an air of
FM7 Bb7 EbMAJ7 FM7 Bb7
Spring___ a - bout it. I can hear___ a lark some -
BbM7 Eb7 AbMAJ7 Db7 Eb/G GbDIM7
where___ be - gin to sing a - bout it; there's no love song
FM7(b5) Bb7 Eb7 AbMAJ7 FM7(b5) AbM7
fin - er,___ but how strange the change from ma - jor to mi - nor
1
EbMAJ7 C7(b9) FM7 Bb7SUS Bb7(b9) Eb6/9 GbDIM7
ev' - ry time___ we say good - bye.
2
FM7 Bb7 F9 Bb7SUS BDIM7 CM7 CM7/Bb AM7(b5) D7
— we say good - bye. Ev' - ry sin - gle
GM7(b5) C7 F7 Bb7 Eb6/9
time we say good - bye.___

FALLING IN LOVE WITH LOVE

WORDS BY LORENZ HART
MUSIC BY RICHARD RODGERS

C
(BbMAJ7 EbMAJ7 Dm7 G7(b9))
Bb BbMAJ7 Bb6 Bb
I fell in love with love one night when the
Cm7 F7
moon was full.
Cm7 F7
I was un - wise with eyes un - ab - le to
BbMAJ7 Bb6
see.
D
(EbMAJ7)
BbMAJ7 Bb6 BbMAJ7
I fell in love with love, with
(Ab9(#11)) (G7(b9)
Bb6 Am7 D7 GMAJ7
love ev - er - last - ing.
)
G7 Cm7 Bdim7 Cm7
But love fell out
1
F7(b9) Bb Gm7 Cm7 F7(b9)
with me.
2
F7 BbMAJ7 Bb6 BbMAJ7 Bb6 Bb
with me

FASCINATING RHYTHM

MUSIC AND LYRICS BY
GEORGE GERSHWIN AND IRA GERSHWIN

FM7 Bb7 BbM7 Eb7 BbM7 Eb7
qui - ver. What a mess you're mak-ing! The neigh-bors want to know why I'm
BbM7 Eb7 BbM7 Eb7 8 Ab6 Ab/G FM7 Bb6 Bb9(#5)
al - ways shak-ing just like a fliv - ver. Each morn - ing I get up with the
(DM7(b5) G7(#9 #5))
Eb6 EbMAJ7 CM7 F7
sun, (start a hop - ping, nev - er stop-ping,) to find at night, no work has been
(FM7 Bb7 GM7 C7(b9)) C
Bb7 C#DIM7 FM7 Bb7 FM7 Bb7
done. I know that once it did-n't mat-ter but now you're do-ing wrong; when you
FM7 Bb7 FM7 Bb7 BbM7 Eb7
start to pat - ter, I'm so un - hap - py. Won't you take a day off? De -
BbM7 Eb7 BbM7 Eb7 BbM7 Eb7 Ab6
cide to run a-long some-where far a - way off, and make it snap - py! Oh, how I
DM7(b5) G7 CM7 F7 FM7 Bb7
long to be the man I used to be! Fas - ci - nat - ing rhy - thm, oh,
1. 2.
FM7 F7 Bb13 Eb6 GM7 C7 Eb6
won't you stop pick - ing on me!" me!"

A FINE ROMANCE

MUSIC BY JEROME KERN
WORDS BY DOROTHY FIELDS

FOOTPRINTS

MEDIUM SWING

BY WAYNE SHORTER

CM11
(BASS PATTERN)
CM11
(BASS CONTINUES SIMILE)
5
FM11
CM11
5
5
(D7)
(F7(#11)
F#M11(♭5)
E7(#9)
F13(#11)
(D♭7)
D7ALT
E7ALT
G7(#5))
A7ALT
1
CM11
2
CM11
CM11
REPEAT AD LIB.

A FOGGY DAY

MUSIC AND LYRICS BY
GEORGE GERSHWIN AND IRA GERSHWIN

FMAJ7 C7(#5) F9 BbMAJ7 BbM6
I viewed the morn - ing with a - larm, the
FMAJ7 D9 G13 G9(#5) C9
Brit - ish Mu - se - um had lost it's charm. How
8
F CM7(b5)/Gb GM7 C13 C13(b9)
long, I won - dered, could this thing last? But the
F FM7/Eb DM7(b5) G13 G7(#5) C9
age of mir - a - cles had - n't passed, for,
CM7/F F13 F13(b9) BbMAJ7 GM7(b5)
sud - den - ly, I saw you there Eb13 and through
F/A Bb6 FMAJ7/C Bb6 DM7 G9
Eb13 Eb13
fog - gy Lon - don town the sun was shin - ing
GM7/C C7
1. F FMAJ7 C7 F7 Bb7 GM7(b5) C7
ev - 'ry - where. A
2. F FMAJ7 C7 F7 Bb7 GM7(b5) BbMAJ7 GM7(b5) FMAJ7
8VA
where.

FOUR

MUSIC BY MILES DAVIS
WORDS BY JON HENDRICKS

A
MEDIUM SWING
EbMAJ7
Of the won - der-ful things that you get out of life there are four_
EbM7
Ab7
FM9
_ and they may not be man - y, but no -
AbM7
Db7
bo - dy needs an - y more.____ Of the man - y
(EbMAJ7)
GM7
F#M7
B7
FM7
facts mak - ing the list of life, truth takes the lead,_
Bb7
(EbMAJ7)
GM7
F#M7
B7
_ and to re - lax know - ing the gist____ of life,____
FM7
Bb7
B
EbMAJ7
it's truth you need. Then the sec - ond is hon - or, and hap -

Ebm7 Ab7
pi - ness makes num - ber three. When you put
Fm9 Abm7 Db7
them to-geth - er you'll know what the last one must be. Ba-by so the
(Ebmaj7)
Gm7 F#m7 B7 Fm7 (Bb7) Dm7(b5) G7(#9)
truth, hon-or and hap - pi - ness and one thing more,
meaning on - ly
meaning love and
1
Gm7 F#m7 Fm7 Bb7 Eb6 (Fm7 Bb7)
won - der-ful, won - der - ful love that-'ll make it four. Of the won -
2
Gm7 F#m7 Fm7 Bb7 Am7(b5)
that's the real score and more that e - nough when times are
D7 Gm7 F#m7
tough and poor they may not com - prise a - lot
Fm7 Bb7 Eb6 Ebm(maj7)
still on - ly got those four. And there ain't no more.

*FREEDOM JAZZ DANCE

BY EDDIE HARRIS

* THIS ARRANGMENT DERIVED FROM COMBINED ELEMENTS FROM THE MILES DAVIS RECORDING, "MILES SMILES", AND THE EDDIE HARRIS RECORDING, "THE BEST OF EDDIE HARRIS".

GEE BABY, AIN'T I GOOD TO YOU

MEDIUM/SLOW SWING

MUSIC BY DON REDMAN
LYRIC BY DON REDMAN AND ANDY RAZAF

A
C7 Ab13 G13 C9
Love___ makes me treat you the way___ that I do,
F7(b9) Bb7 Eb6 DM7 G7(#5) C7 Ab13
gee ba-by, ain't I good_ to you. There's noth - in' too good for a
G13 C9 F7(b9) Bb7 Eb6 BbM7 Eb7
girl___ that's so true, gee ba-by, ain't I good_ to you.
B
Ab ADIM7 Eb/Bb BbM7 Eb7
Bought you a fur coat for Christ - mas, a dia - mond ring,___
C
Ab ADIM7 DM7(b5) G7(b9) C7 Ab13
a Cad-il-lac car, an' ev-'ry-thing.___ Love___ makes me treat you the
G13 C9 F7(b9) Bb7 Eb6 DM7 G7(#5) Eb6
way___ that I do, gee ba-by, ain't I good_ to you. you.

GENTLE RAIN

MEDIUM BALLAD / BOSSA

MUSIC BY LUIZ BONFA
WORDS BY MATT DUBEY

GIANT STEPS

FAST SWING

BY JOHN COLTRANE

BMAJ7
D7
GMAJ7
Bb7
EbMAJ7
AM7
D7
GMAJ7
Bb7
EbMAJ7
F#7
BMAJ7
FM7
Bb7
EbMAJ7
AM7
D7
GMAJ7
C#M7
F#7
BMAJ7
FM7
Bb7
1
EbMAJ7
C#M7
F#7
2
EbMAJ7

THE GIRL FROM IPANEMA

MUSIC BY ANTONIO CARLOS JOBIM
ORIGINAL WORDS BY VINICIUS DE MORAES
ENGLISH WORDS BY NORMAN GIMBEL

BOSSA NOVA

GIRL TALK

WORDS BY BOBBY TROUP
MUSIC BY NEAL HEFTI

SLOW SWING

GOOD BAIT

MEDIUM BE-BOP

WORDS & MUSIC BY
TADD DAMERON AND COUNT BASIE

GROOVIN' HIGH

MUSIC BY JOHN "DIZZY" GILLESPIE

BE-BOP
Eb AM7 D7 AM7 D7
Eb GM7 C7 GM7 C7
F7 FM7 Bb7 FM7 Bb7
EbMAJ7 GM7 F#M7 FM7 E7
Eb AM7 D7 AM7 D7
Eb GM7 C7 GM7 C7
F7 FM7 Bb7 FM7 Bb7
FM7 AbM7 Db7 Eb6 Gb7 FM7 E7 Eb6

GOOD MORNING, HEARTACHE

MEDIUM BALLAD

WORDS AND MUSIC BY DAN FISHER,
ERVIN DRAKE AND IRENE HIGGINBOTHAM

GM7 C7(#9 #5) C7(#5) FMAJ7
B
"Good morn - ing heart - ache, what's new?"
EM11 A7(#9 #5) DM6 EM11 A7
Stop haunt - ing me now, can't shake you no -
DMAJ7 DM11 G7(#9 #5) CMAJ7
how. Just leave me a - lone. I've
C#M11 F#7 CM11 F7
got those Mon - day blues straight through Sun - day blues.
C
CM Ab/C CM6 CM7
Good morn - ing heart - ache, here we go a - gain.
FMAJ7 BbMAJ7 AM7(b5) Eb7 D7(b9)
Good morn - ing heart - ache you're the one who knew me when.
GM7 BbM(MAJ7) Eb9 AM7 AbM7 Db9
Might as well get used to you hang - in' a - round.
GM7 C13 FMAJ7
Good morn - ing heart - ache, sit down.

HAVE YOU MET MISS JONES?

WORDS BY LORENZ HART
MUSIC BY RICHARD RODGERS

(Abm7 Db7 Gm7 C7(b9))
Gm7 C7(b9) Fmaj7
me. Then I said "Miss
(F#dim7)
Am7 D7(b9) Gm7 C7sus C7
Jones, you're a girl who un - der - stands,
(Gm7 C7 Cm7 F7)
Am7 Dm7 G9 Cm7 F7(b9)
I'm a man who must be free." And all at
B
Bbmaj7 Abm7 Db7 Gbmaj9 Em7 A7
once I lost my breath, and all at once was scared to death, and all at
(Bm7)
Dmaj7 Abm9 Db7 Gbmaj9 Gm7 C7
once I owned the earth and sky.
C
(Fmaj7 F#dim7)
Fmaj7 Bb9 Am7 D7(b9) Gm7
Now I've met Miss Jones, and we'll go on
(Bb9)
C7sus C9 Am7 D7 Gm7 C7(b9)
meet - ing till we die, Miss Jones and
1 F Gm7 C7(b9)
I.
2 F
I.

HERE'S THAT RAINY DAY

WORDS BY JOHNNY BURKE
MUSIC BY JIMMY VAN HEUSEN

BALLAD

HONEYSUCKLE ROSE

MUSIC BY THOMAS "FATS" WALLER
WORDS BY ANDY RAZAF

HIT THAT JIVE JACK

BY JOHNNY ALSTON AND
CAMPBELL 'SKEETS' TOLBERT

AM7 D7 C G9 E7 AM7 D7
(BM7) to give you five (Sha-dee-a-dah) Hit that jive Jack, and
G9 E7 AM7 D7 G G7/B
put it in your pock-et 'til I get back. I'm go-in' down town to
C6 C#oM7 G/D E7(#9) AM7 D7 G
see your man, and I ain't got time to shake your hand.
D
G9 E7 AM7 D7 G9 E7
Hit that jive Jack and put it in your pock-et 'til
AM7 D7 G C6 C#oM7
I get back. I'm go-in' down town to see your man and I
G/B D7 G G9 E7
ain't got time to shake your hand. Hit that jive
AM7 D7 G9 E7 AM7 D7
Jack and put it in your pock-et 'til I get back. I'm-
G G7/B C6 C#oM7 G/D
go-in' down town to see your man and I ain't got time to

D7 G
E
Dm9 G13 Cmaj7
shake your hand. Stand - in' on the cor - ner all full of jive.
A6
But you know that you're my boy so I'm forced
Am7 D
F
G9 E7
to give you five. (Sha - dee - a - dah) Hit that jive
Am7 D7 G9 E7 Am7 D7
Jack and put it in your pock - et 'til I get back. I'm
G G7/B C6 C#dim7 G/D D7 G
go - in' down town to see your man and I ain't got time to shake your hand.
G
Gm7
Hit that jive Jack, ba - na - na, put it in your pock - et.
Hit that jive Jack, ba - na - na, put it in your pock - et.
H
Bb7
Hit that jive Jack, ba - na - na, put it in your pock - et.

Hit that jive Jack, ba-na-na, put it in your pock-et.
I
Fm7
Bb7
Ebmaj7
VOCAL AD LIB.
C7
Cm7
F13
J
Bb9
G7
Cm7
F7
Bb9
G7
Hit that jive Jack and put it in your pock - et 'til
Cm7
F7
Bb
Bb7/D
E6
Edim7
I get back. I'm go - in' down town to see your man___ and I
N.C.
C9(#11)
Ebm(maj7)
ain't got time, I ain't got time, I
Cm9
Ebm7
N.C.
ain't got time to shake your hand.___ Gon - na put it in your pock - et 'til
Bb6
Bb
I get back. Hit that jive Jack.

HOT HOUSE

UP-TEMPO BE-BOP

WORDS & MUSIC BY TADD DAMERON

HOW HIGH THE MOON

WORDS BY NANCY HAMILTON
MUSIC BY MORGAN LEWIS

HOW INSENSITIVE

MUSIC BY ANTONIO CARLOS JOBIM
ORIGINAL WORDS BY VINICIUS DE MORAES
ENGLISH WORDS BY NORMAN GIMBEL

BOSSA NOVA
A
DM7
A7(b9)/C#
How insensitive I must have seemed
Now {he's / she's} gone away and I'm alone
CM6
G7/B
when {he / she} told me that {he / she} loved me.
with the mem-'ry of {his / her} last look.
BbMAJ7
EbMAJ7
How unmoved and cold I must have seemed
Vague and drawn and sad, I see it still,
EM7(b5)
A7(#5)
DM7
when {he / she} told me so sincerely.
all {his / her} heart-break in that last look.
B
F7/C
BM7(b5)
BbMAJ7
Why, {he / she} must have asked, did I just turn and
How, {he / she} must have asked, could I just turn and
(A7SUS(b9))
GM7
DM7
F7/C
stare in icy silence? What was I to say?
stare in icy silence? What was I to do?
BM11
E7(b9)
(BbMAJ7)
GM6/Bb
(EM7(b5)
A7(b9)
A7(b9))
What can you say when a love affair is o-
What can you do when a love affair is o-
1
DM7
A7(#9)
ver?
2
DM7
ver?

(I Don't Stand) A Ghost of a Chance (With You)

Words by Bing Crosby and Ned Washington
Music by Victor Young

HOW LONG HAS THIS BEEN GOING ON?

MUSIC AND LYRICS BY
GEORGE GERSHWIN AND IRA GERSHWIN

FREELY
VERSE:

GMAJ7 EM7 AM7 D7(♭9) G6 EM7 AM7 D7SUS
He: As a tot when I trot-ted in lit-tle vel-vet pan - ties,
She: 'Neath the stars at ba - zaars of-ten I've had to car - ess men.
G♯M7(♭5) C♯7 F♯7(♯9 ♯5) F♯7(♭9) BM BM(MAJ7) E7SUS E7
I was kissed by my sis - ters, my cou-sins and my aunt - ies.
Five or ten dol-lars, then I'd col-lect from all those yes men.
AM7 AM/G B7/F♯ E7(♭9 ♯5) E7(♭9) AM7 E7SUS(♭9) AM7
Sad to tell, it was hell, an in - fer - no worse than Dan - te's.
Don't be sad I must add that they meant no more than chess men.
A7 EM9 A13 AM7 D7
So my dear, I swore, "Nev - er, nev - er more!"
Dar - ling, can't you see t'was for char - i - ty?
GMAJ7 EM7 AM7 D7(♭9) G6 EM7 AM7 D7SUS
On my list I in - sis - ted that kiss - ing must be crossed out.
Though these lips have made slips it was nev - er real - ly se - rious.
BM BM6 C♯7 F♯7(♯9 ♯5) F♯7(♭9) BM BM/A G♯M7(♭5)
Now I find I was blind, and oh la - dy how I've lost out!
Who'd a' thought I'd be brought to a state that's so de - li - rious?
A
CHORUS:
BALLAD OR MEDIUM
(AM7 A♭DIM7 AM7 D7 DM G13 CMAJ9 F7SUS)
D9 DDIM7 D9 G13 C13 CM7
I could cry salt - y tears; where have I been all these years?
I could cry salt - y tears; where have I been all these years?

(Abdim7 Am7 Eb9 D13 Bm7 E7(b9))
G/B Bbdim7 Am7 D7 G7 Cmaj7 D13 Gmaj7
Lit - tle wow, tell me now, how long has this been go - ing on?
List - en you, tell me do, how long has this been go - ing on?
(Am7 Abdim7 Am7 D7 Dm G13 Cmaj9 F7sus)
D9 Ddim7 D9 G13 C13 Cm7
There were chills up my spine, and some thrills I can't de - fine.
What a kick! How I buzz! Boy, you click as no - one does!
(Abdim7 Am7 Eb9 D13)
G/B Bbdim7 Am7 D7 G7 Cmaj7 D13 G6 Dm7 G7
Lis - ten sweet, I re - peat: how long has this been go - ing on?
Hear me sweet, I re - peat: how long has this been go - ing on?
C
(C#m7(b5) F#7(b9))
Cmaj7 F9 Cmaj7 F9 Cmaj7 F7 Cmaj7 A9
Oh I feel that I could melt; in - to heav - en I'm hurled.
Dear when in your arms I creep, that di - vine ren - dez - vous.
Bm7 C#m7(b5) F#7(b9) Bm7 C#m7(b5) F#7(b9) Bm7 C#m7(b5) F#7(b9) Bm7 Bb7(#5)
I know how Co - lum - bus felt, find - ing an - oth - er world.
Don't wake me if I'm a - sleep. Let me dream that it's true.
D
(Am7 Abdim7 Am7 D7 Dm G13
D9 Ddim7 D9 G13
Kiss me once, then once more. What a dunce I
Kiss me twice, then once more. That makes thrice, let's
Cmaj9 F7sus) (Abdim7
C13 Cm7 G/B Bbdim7 Am7 D7 G7
was be - fore.
make it four!
What a break! For heav - en's sake! How
Am7 Eb9 D13)
Cmaj7 D13
1 G6 E7(b9 #5) Optional DC
2 G6
long has this be go - ing on?

I CAN'T GET STARTED

WORDS BY IRA GERSHWIN
MUSIC BY VERNON DUKE

(Bm7 E7 B♭m7 E♭7 Am7 D7 A♭m7 D♭7)
E7 Am7 D13 G7sus Cmaj7 Am7
mov - ies want me to star; I've got a house, a show place, but
ads all fea - ture my smiles the As - tor bilts I vis - it, but
Dm7 G7(♭9) Cmaj7 Fm6 Cmaj7
I get no place with you. You're so su -
say what is it with you? When first we
B
Em7 A7 Em7 A7 Dmaj7 (G9 F♯m7 Em7 A7sus)
preme, ly - rics I write of you, scheme just for a sight of you,
met, how you e - la - ted me Pet, you dev - as - tat - ed me!
Dm7 G9 Dm7 G7 (Cmaj7 A9 D9 G7sus) Em7 E♭dim7 Dm7 G7sus
dream both day and night of you and what good does it do? In nine - teen
Yet, now you've de - flat - ed me till you're my Wa - ter - loo. I've sold my
C
Cmaj7 Am7 Dm7 G7 (Bm7 E7 B♭m7 E♭7) E7 Am7
twen - ty nine I sold short; in En - gland I'm pre - sen - ted at
kiss - es at a ba - zaar, and af - ter me they've named a ci
(Am7 D7 A♭m7 D♭7) D13 G7sus Cmaj7 A7(♭9 ♯5) Dm9 G7
court, but you've got me down - heart - ed 'cause I can't get star - ted with
gar; but late - ly how I've smart - ed 'cause I can't get start - ed with
1 C6/9 A7(♯5) Dm7 G7 2 C6/9
you. I do a you.

I COULD WRITE A BOOK

Words by LORENZ HART
Music by RICHARD RODGERS

CMAJ7 AM7 DM11 G7-13 G7/F
way you walk and whis - per and look. I could
B
C/E E♭DIM7 DM7 G7 F#M7(♭5) B7(♭9) EM7
write a pre - face on how we met, so the
(AM7 D7SUS)
G/B B♭DIM7 AM7 D7 DM11 G7
world would nev - er for - get. And the
C
CMAJ7 AM7 DM7 G13 CMAJ7 AM7 DM7 G7
sim - ple se - cret of the plot is just to
CMAJ7 AM7 DM11 G7 G7/F
tell them that I love you a lot. Then the
D
C/E E♭DIM7 DM7 G7 GM7 C7(♭9) FMAJ7 B♭13 EM7 A7(♭9)
world dis - cov - ers as my book ends, how to make two
1 2
DM7 G7(♭9) C6/9 DM7 G7 C6/9
lov - ers of friends. If they friends.

I GOT IT BAD

WORDS & MUSIC BY
DUKE ELLINGTON AND PAUL WEBSTER

AM7 B7(#5) E7 A7 D13 G6 EM7 AM7 D7
A7
I got it bad and that ain't good!
D7
(GMAJ7 CMAJ7)
GDIM7 G C/G G B7 EM7 A9 EM7 A9
My poor heart is sen - ti - men - tal, not made of wood.
And the things I tell my pil - low no wom - an should.
(G6 Db7(b5))
AM7 B7(#5) E7 A7 D13 G6 C#DIM7 DM7 G7 G7(#5)
I got it bad and that ain't good!
But
Tho'
B
(CM7 F7)
C6 F7
when the week - end's o - ver and Mon - day rolls a - round, I
folks with good in - ten - tions tell me to save my tears. I'm
(F7)
GMAJ7 BM7 E7 AM7 Eb7(#5) D7(b9)
end up like I start out, just cry - in' my heart out.
glad I'm mad a - bout him. I can't live with - out him.
D7
C
(GMAJ7 CMAJ7)
(Bb9)
GDIM7 G C/G G B7 EM7 A9 EM7 A9
He don't love me like I love him. No - bo - dy could.
Lord a - bove me, make him love me the way he should.
(BM7 Bb7 AM7 Ab9)
AM7 B7(#5) E7 A7 D13 G6 EM7 AM7 D7 G6
1
2
I got it bad and that ain't good.
good.

I GOT RHYTHM

Music and Lyrics by
GEORGE GERSHWIN and IRA GERSHWIN

(Eb7 EDIM7)
Bb Bb7/D CM7 F7 Bb/F F7 Bb F7
I got my man, who could ask for an-y-thing more?
(DM7)
Bb GM7 CM7 F7 Bb GM7 CM7 F7
I got dais - ies in green pas - tures,
(Eb7 EDIM7)
Bb Bb7/D CM7 F7 Bb/F F7 Bb
I got my man, who could ask for an-y-thing more?
B
D7 G7
Old Man Trou - ble, I don't mind him,
C7 F7
you won't find him 'round my door.
C
(DM7)
Bb GM7 CM7 F7 Bb GM7 CM7 F7
I got star - light, I got sweet dreams,
(Eb7 EDIM7)
Bb Bb7/D CM7 F7
I got my man, who
1
Bb/F F7 Bb F7
could ask for an-y-thing more?
2
Bb/F Ab7 G7 C7 F7 Bb
ask for an-y-thing more? Who could ask for an-y-thing more?

I GOTTA RIGHT TO SING THE BLUES

SLOW AND BLUESY

WORDS BY TED KOEHLER
MUSIC BY HAROLD ARLEN

VERSE:
Bb6 (Eb7) F7 Bb6
I don't care who knows I am blue. My song
Dm7 Gm7 C7(b9) (B13) F7(#9) Bb6 G7(b9 #5) C7(b9 #5) F9
would-n't take long to give my heart a-way. I know
Bb6 (Eb7) F7 Bb6
it's plain my heart's in pain. My song
Dm7 Gm7 C7(b9) F7sus Bb6 F7sus Bb6
could-n't be-long to some-one feel-ing gay. I got-ta
A
CHORUS:
Gm7 C9 Gm7 C9 (Cm7) F7 F7(#5)
right to sing the blues, I got-ta right to feel low down.
Fm7 Bb9 Fm7 Bb9
I got-ta right to hang a-round, down a-round the

Dm7(b5) G7 Gm7 C9
riv - er. A cer - tain man in this old town
Gm7 C9 Cm9 F13 Cm7 F13
keeps drag - ging my poor heart a - round. All I
(Cm7 Dbdim7 Bb6/D Eb6 Edim7 Bb G7)
Bb6 F9/Bb Bbdim7 Bb6 Cm7/Bb Bbdim7 F7/Bb Bb6
see for me is mis - e - ry. I got - ta
8
Gm7 C9 Gm7 C9 Cm7 (Db7) F7(#5)
right to sing the blues, I got - ta right to moan and sigh.
(Gbmaj7 F9(#5)) Fm7 Bb9 Fm7 Bb9 (Ebm7 Ab13) Dm7(b5)
I got - ta right to sit and cry down a - round the riv
(Dm7 G7) G7 Gm7 C9 Gm7 C9 (Ab7(#11)) Ebm(maj7)
er. I know the deep blue sea will soon be cal - ling me.
G- C9
Gm7 C9 Cm7 (Gb13 F13) F7(b9)
It must be love, say what you choose, I got - ta right to sing the blues.
1 2
Bb6 Dm7 G13 Bb6
I got - ta

I HEAR A RHAPSODY

WORDS & MUSIC BY GEORGE FRAGOS, JACK BAKER AND DICK GASPARRE

I Let a Song Go Out of My Heart

BY DUKE ELLINGTON, IRVING MILLS,
HENRY NEMO AND JOHN REDMOND

MEDIUM SWING

I LOVE PARIS

WORDS AND MUSIC BY COLE PORTER

VERSE:
FREELY
C
F6
Ev - 'ry time I look down on this time - less town, wheth - er
DM7
G13
C
DM7
G13
blue or grey be her skies, wheth - er
EM7(b5)
A7
AM11
D7
loud be her cheers, or wheth - er soft be her tears, more and
DM7(b5)
G13
C
G7(b9 #5)
more do I re - al - ize, that,
A
MED / BRIGHT
CHORUS:
CM
I love Par - is in the spring - time.
DM7(b5)
G7(b9)
I love Par - is in the fall.
DM7(b5)
G7(b9)
DM7(b5)
G7(b9)
I love Par - is in the win - ter, when it driz - zles.

Dm7(♭5) G7(♭9 ♯5) Cm G7
I love Par - is in the sum - mer, when it siz - zles.
8
C Dm7 G13 Cmaj7 C6
I love Par - is ev - 'ry mo - ment,
Dm7 G13 C Em7 E♭dim7
ev - 'ry mo - ment of the
Dm11 G13 Fmaj7 F♯dim7
year. I love Par - is.
C/G Em7 A7 Dm7
Why, oh why, do I love Par - is? Be - cause my
G13 C Dm7(♭5) G7(♭9) Dm7
love is near. Be - cause my
Em7 A7 Dm11 Dm7/G
love be - cause my love is
C
near.

I LOVE YOU

WORDS & MUSIC BY COLE PORTER

FREELY
A
VERSE:
C7(#5) FM D♭7 GM7
If a love song I could on - ly write,
C7(#5) D♭MAJ7 B♭M7 GM7(♭5) C7(♭9)
a song with words and mu - sic di - vine, I would
GM7(♭5) C7(♭9) FM DM7(♭5)
se - re - nade you ev' - ry night, till you'd re - lent and con -
B
G7 C7SUS C7(♭9) FMAJ7
sent to be mine. But a - las, just an
F+ F6 F9 B♭MAJ7 D7(♭9 #5)
am - a - teur am I, and so I'll not be sur - prised, my
GM7 BM7(♭5) B♭9(#11) A13 A7(#5)
dear, if you smile and po - lite - ly pass it by.
D9 G9 C7SUS C7(♭9) F6
When this, my first love song you hear. "I

MEDIUM SWING/LATIN
C
CHORUS:
Gm7(b5) C7(b9) Fmaj7 Am7 D7(b9) Gm9
love you," hums the A - pril breeze. "I love you,"
C7 F6 Am7 D7 Gm7(b5) C7(b9)
e - cho the hills. "I love you," the gol - den
(E/F Fmaj7)
Fmaj7 Bm7 E7sus(b9) Amaj7 Bm7 E7(b9) Amaj7
dawn a - grees as once more she sees da - fo - dils.
D
D9 Gm7 C7sus C7 (A/F) Fmaj7
It's spring a - gain and birds on the wing a - gain
(Fmaj7)
Am7(b5) D7(b9 #5) G13 G7(#5) C7sus C7(b9)
start to sing a - gain the old mel - o - dy. "I
E
(Am7(b5) D7(#9 #5))
Gm7(b5) C7(b9) Fmaj7 Am7 D7(b9) G7(#11) G7
love you", that's the song of songs, and it all be-longs to
C7sus C13(b9) 1 F6/9 (Am7 D7) 2 F6/9 Bb6/F
you and me. I me. And it all be -
Fmaj9 Bbm6/F F6
longs to you and me.

I MISS YOU SO

MEDIUM BALLAD

BY JIMMY HENDERSON, BERTHA SCOTT AND SID ROBIN

I SHOULD CARE

MEDIUM SWING

WORDS AND MUSIC BY SAMMY CAHN, AXEL STORDAHL AND PAUL WESTON

I'LL BE AROUND

WORDS AND MUSIC BY ALEC WILDER

MEDIUM BALLAD

I'LL REMEMBER APRIL

MED / BRIGHT

WORDS AND MUSIC BY DON RAYE, GENE DE PAUL AND PAT JOHNSTON

I'M AN ERRAND GIRL FOR RHYTHM

BY NAT KING COLE

FREELY
A
FMAJ7
CMAJ9
Here's some - thing that I'd like to bring to you, wrapped all in cell - o -
FAST SWING
EbDIM7
B
D7
Db7
phane, de - signed for you. Tell you what it's all a - bout; it is with - out
C7
D9
3
a doubt a swing in the lat - est style, a ser - vice with
G13
C
C
A7
D9
G13
EM
A7(#5)
a smile. If you want to swing and shout kick your heels and
DM9
G13
C
E7
A7
gad a - bout. I'm an er - rand girl for rhy - thm. Send

D9 G13 C A7 D9 G13 Em7 A7(♭5)
me. Just get hip and fol-low through. I'll de - li - ver
Dm9 G13 C E7 A7 D7 G13 C
straight to you. I'm an er-rand girl for rhy - thm. Send me.
D
E6 A7 D7
You can al-ways find me down at Smok-ey Joe's. That's where all the
G13 E C A7 D9 G13
hip and groov - y peo-ple go. If you want va - ri - e - ty take a
Em7 A7(♯5) Dm9 G13 C B7
tip and call for me. I'm an er - rand girl for rhy -
1 2
B♭7 A7 D7 G13 C G13 D7 G13 C
thm. Send me. Send me.

I'M BEGINNING TO SEE THE LIGHT

MEDIUM SWING

BY DUKE ELLINGTON, HARRY JAMES,
JOHNNY HODGES AND DON GEORGE

IMPRESSIONS

FAST SWING

BY JOHN COLTRANE

I'VE GOT YOU UNDER MY SKIN

WORDS & MUSIC BY COLE PORTER

B
Fm7 Bb11 EbMAJ7 Eb6
got you under my skin. I'd
(Fm7) Fm7/Eb (Bb7(b9)) Bb7/Eb EbMAJ7 (Gm7 C7(b9)) Eb7
sac-ri-fice an-y-thing, come what might, for the sake of hav-ing you near. In spite of a
(Fm7) Fm7/Eb (Bb7(b9)) Fm7(b5)/Eb Gm7 Gb7 Fm11 Bb13
warn-ing voice that comes in the night and re-peats and re-peats in my ear: "Don't you
C
Cm7 Fm7 Bb7(#5) EbMAJ7 Gm7 GbDIM7
know, lit-tle fool, you nev-er can win. Use your men-
Fm11 Bb13 EbMAJ7
tal-i-ty. Wake up to re-al-i-ty."
Bbm7 Eb7(b9) Ab6 Abm6
But each time I do, just the thought of you makes me
Eb6/Bb Gm7(b5) C7(b9) Fm9 Bb13
stop, be-fore I be-gin, 'cause I've got you un-der my
1 Eb Gm7 C7(b9)
skin. I've
2 Eb Bb11 Eb
skin.

In a Mellow Tone

Music by Duke Ellington

Medium Swing
A
N.C.
Bb7
Eb7
(Abmaj7)
Ab6
In a mel-low tone, feel-in' fan-cy free.
Ebm7
Ab7
Dbmaj7
And I'm not a - lone, I've got com-pa - ny. Ev-'ry-thing's O. K.
Db6
(Dbm6)
Gb13
(Abmaj7 Gb7)
Ab6
F9
the live - long day. With this mel-low song
Bb7
(Ebdim7 Eb7)
Eb7
F7
I can't go wrong. In a mel-low tone,
B
Bb7
Eb7
(Abmaj7)
Ab6
Ebm7
that's the way to live. If you mope and groan,
Ab7
Dbmaj7
Db7
some-thing's got to give. So go your way
Ddim7
Ab6/Eb
F7(b5)
Bb7
and laugh and play. There's joy un - known
Eb7
1
Ab6
F7
2
Ab6
in a mel-low tone. In a mel-low tone,

IN A SENTIMENTAL MOOD

BY DUKE ELLINGTON, IRVING MILLS
AND MANNY KURTZ

IN WALKED BUD

BY THELONIUS MONK

MEDIUM SWING
A
FM
FM(MAJ7)
FM7
Bb7
Eb7
Ab6
F7
BbM7
Eb7
Ab6
1
GM7(b5)
C7
2
B
FM7
Db7
FM7
Db7
C
FM
FM(MAJ7)
FM7
Bb7
Eb7
Ab6
F7
BbM7
Eb7
Ab6
1
GM7(b5)
C7
2
Gb6/9

IN YOUR OWN SWEET WAY

WORDS AND MUSIC BY DAVE BRUBECK

INVITATION

BALLAD / MEDIUM SWING / LATIN

Music by BRONISLAU KAPER
Lyrics by PAUL FRANCIS WEBSTER

D7(♭9 ♯5)
GM9
al-ways your eyes smile that strange in-vi - ta - tion. Then you are
E♭9(♯11)
D7(♭9)
G7(♯5)
G7
gone. Where, oh, where have you gone? How
D
CM9
long must I stay in a world of il - lu - sion, be where you
(F7(♯9))
F13
B♭7(♭9 ♭5)
B♭13
are, so near yet so far a - part,
E
E♭M9
B9(♯11)
hop - ing you'll say, with a warm in - vi - ta - tion,
F7(♯9)
B♭7(♯9)
"Where have you been? Dar - ling come in, come in - to my
1
E♭M(MAJ7)
D7(♭9 ♯5)
G7(♭9)
heart."
2
E♭M(MAJ7)
heart."

IS YOU IS, OR IS YOU AIN'T

(MA' BABY?)

MEDIUM BLUESY

WORDS AND MUSIC BY BILLY AUSTIN AND LOUIS JORDAN

FM7 FM7/Ab EM7(b5)/G FM7
you'se is still my ba - by, ba - by.
Bb7 Eb7 Ab6/9 EbM7 Ab7(#5)
Seems my flame in your heart's done gone out.
A
C
DbMAJ7 DbM7 Ab6/9
wo - man is
man is just
a crea - ture that has al - ways been strange. Just
Db6/9 Ab/C GM7(b5) C7(#9)
when you're sure of one you find
she's
he's
gone and made a change.
D
FM7 EM7(b5)/G FM7/Ab EM7(b5)/G FM7
Is you is or is you ain't my ba - by?
Bb7 Eb7 Gb7(#11)
May be ba - by's found some - bod - y new;
F7 BbM9 Eb7 Ab6/9 Db7 C7
or is ma' ba - by still ma' ba - by true?
Eb7 Ab6/9
still ma' ba - by true?

THE ISLAND

(Comecar De Novo)

By Alan and Marilyn Bergman,
Ivan Lins and Vitor Martins

Moderate Latin/Ballad

* Vocal usually sung one octave lower.

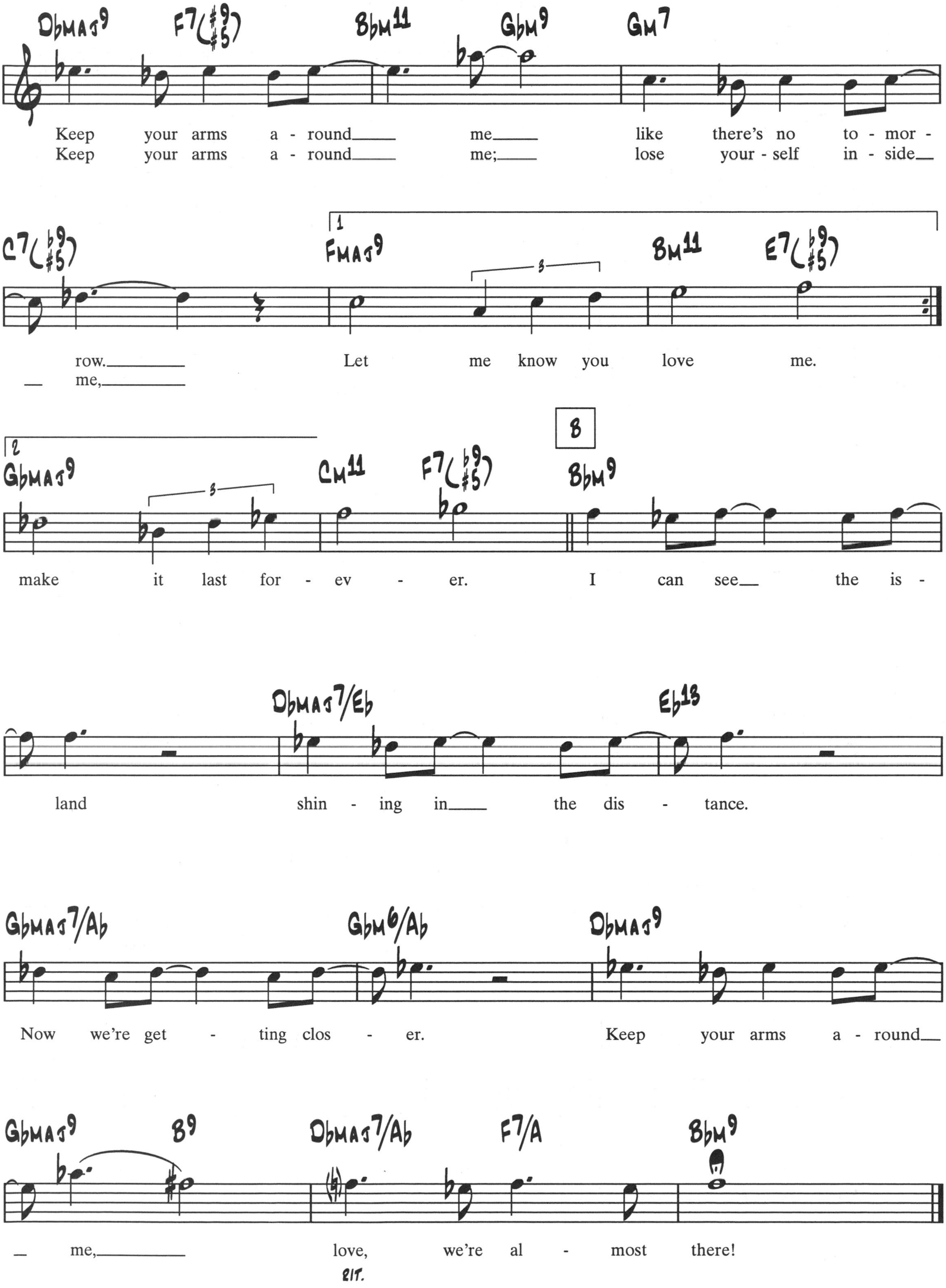
DbMAJ9 F7(#9 #5) BbM11 GbM9 GM7
Keep your arms a - round me like there's no to - mor -
Keep your arms a - round me; lose your - self in - side
C7(b9 #5) FMAJ9 BM11 E7(b9 #5)
row. Let me know you love me.
me,
GbMAJ9 CM11 F7(b9 #5) BbM9
make it last for - ev - er. I can see the is -
8
DbMAJ7/Eb Eb13
land shin - ing in the dis - tance.
GbMAJ7/Ab GbM6/Ab DbMAJ9
Now we're get - ting clos - er. Keep your arms a - round
GbMAJ9 B9 DbMAJ7/Ab F7/A BbM9
me, love, we're al - most there!
RIT.

IT DON'T MEAN A THING
(IF IT AIN'T GOT THAT SWING)

MUSIC BY DUKE ELLINGTON
WORDS BY IRVING MILLS

(Gm Gm/F# Gm/F Gm/E Eb7 D7 G7(#5))
Gm Gm(maj7) Gm7 Gm6
don't mean a thing, all you got to do is sing,
(Em7(b5) Ebm6 Bb6/D C7 F7 Bb6)
C7 F7 Bb6
doo wah, doo wah, doo wah, doo wah, doo wah, doo wah, doo wah, doo wah. It
B
Fm7 Bb7 Eb6
makes no diff-'rence if it's sweet or hot; just
Gm7 C7 F7 D7
give that rhy-thm ev - 'ry thing you got. It
C
(Gm Gm/F# Gm/F Gm/E Eb7 D7)
Gm Gm(maj7) Gm7
don't mean a thing if it ain't got that swing,
(C7 C#dim7 Bb6/D G7(#9 #5))
Gm6 C7 F7
doo wah, doo wah, doo wah, doo wah, doo wah,
1.
(Cm7 F7 Bb6 D7(#5))
Bb6
doo wah, doo wah, doo wah. It
2
(Cm7 F7 Bb6)
Bb6
doo wah, doo wah, doo wah.

IT'S A RAGGY WALTZ

SWINGING JAZZ WALTZ

WORDS AND MUSIC BY DAVE BRUBECK

IT'S ONLY A PAPER MOON

MED / BRIGHT

WORDS BY BILLY ROSE AND E.Y. HARBURG
MUSIC BY HAROLD ARLEN

A
Say, it's on-ly a pa-per moon, sail-ing o-ver a card-board sea.
But it would-n't be make be-lieve if you be-lieved in me.
Yes, it's on-ly a can-vas sky, hang-ing o-ver a mus-lin tree.
But it would-n't be make be-lieve if you be-lieved in me. With-
B
out your love, it's a hon-ky-tonk pa-rade; With-
out your love, it's a mel-o-dy played in a pen-ny ar-cade.
C
It's a Bar-num and Bai-ley world, just as phon-y as it can be. But it would-n't be
make be-lieve if you be-lieved in me. be-lieved in me.

JAVA JIVE

WORDS BY MILTON DRAKE
MUSIC BY BEN OAKLAND

JUST FRIENDS

MUSIC BY JOHN KLENNER
LYRIC BY SAM M. LEWIS

JOSIE

BY WALTER BECKER AND DONALD FAGEN

MEDIUM JAZZ ROCK
N.C.
C/F F#7(#9) D/G Abmaj13
Em7
A
VERSE:
Em7
1. We're gon-na
break out the hats and hoo - ters when Jo-sie comes home.
2. Jo, would you love to scrap - ple? She'll nev - er say no.
3. (INST. SOLO AD LIB. . . .
We're gon-na rev-up the motor - scoot - ers when Jo - sie comes
We're gon-na shine up the bat-tle ap - ple, we'll shake them all
Dmaj7 G/C D/G C/F Em7
home to stay we're gon-na park in the street, sleep on the beach and make
down to-night we're gon-na mix in the street, strike at the stroke of mid -
A7 G/C D/G C/F
- it. Throw down the jam 'til the girls say "When."
night. Dance on the bones 'til the girls say "When."
Em7 D/G E/A Em7
Lay down the law and break it when Jo - sie comes home.
Pick - up what's left by day - light when Jo - sie comes home.
...3RD TIME END SOLO)

B
CHORUS:
C/F F#7(#9) B7(#5) EM7 C/F
1.3. When Jo - sie comes home so good. She's the pride
2. When Jo - sie comes home so bad. She's the best
F#7(#9) B7(#5) EM7 A7 AM7 D9
of the neigh - bor - hood.
friend we nev - er had.
She's the raw flame, the
TO CODA
1
GMAJ7 CMAJ7 F#7(#9) B7(#9)
live wire. She prays like a Ro - man with her eyes on fire.
EM7
2
B7(#9)
eyes on fire.
C
EM7
F#7(#9) B7(#9) D.S. AL CODA
CODA B7(#9) N.C.
eyes on fire.
C/F F#7(#9) D/G AbMAJ13 EM7 REPEAT AD LIB. AND FADE

KID CHARLEMAGNE

MEDIUM ROCK

WORDS AND MUSIC BY
WALTER BECKER AND DONALD FAGEN

Verse 2
On the hill the stuff was laced with kerosene,
But yours was kitchen clean.
Everyone stopped to stare at your technicolor motor home.
Every A-frame had your number on the wall,
You must've had it all,
You'd go to L.A. on a dare, and you'd go it alone.
Could you live forever? Could you see the day,
Could you feel your whole world fall apart and fade away?
Get along, get along, Kid Charlemagne,
Get along, Kid Charlemagne.

Verse 3
Now your patrons have all left you in the red,
Your low-rent friends are dead.
This life can be very strange.
All those day-glo freaks who used to paint the face;
They've joined the human race.
Some things will never change.
Son, you are mistaken. You are obsolete.
Look at all the white men on the street.
Get along, get along, Kid Charlemagne,
Get along, Kid Charlemagne.

Verse 4
Clean this mess up else we'll all end up in jail.
Those test-tubes and the scale.
Just get it all out of here.
Is there gas in the car?
Yes, there's gas in the car.
I think the people down the hall know who you are.
Careful what you carry, 'cause the man is wise.
You are still an outlaw in their eyes.
Get along, get along, Kid Charlemagne,
Get along, Kid Charlemagne.

LA FIESTA

MODERATE FLAMENCO STYLE, IN 1

BY CHICK COREA

C
E F G F
1 F E
2 F E
AMAJ7
BM7/A AMAJ7 BM7/A AMAJ7 BM7/A AMAJ7 BM7/A
D
AMAJ7 C#7 DMAJ7 D#DIM7 A/E
FDIM7 F#M7 B7 E7 A
DMAJ7 C#M7 F#7 B7
E7 AMAJ7
C#7 DMAJ7 D#DIM7 A/E FDIM7
F#M7 B7 E7 AMAJ7 DMAJ7

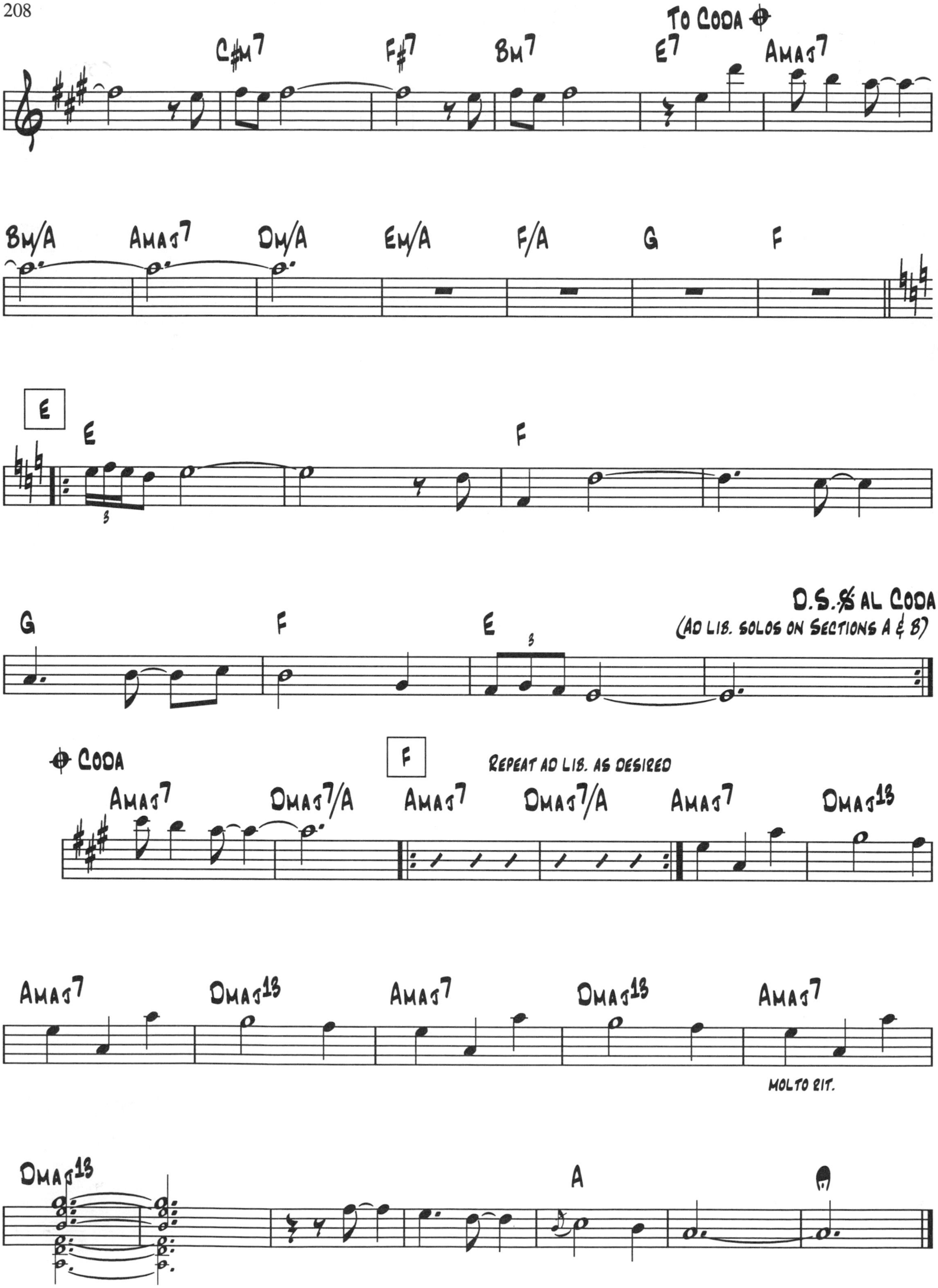
TO CODA
C#M7
F#7
BM7
E7
AMAJ7
BM/A
AMAJ7
DM/A
EM/A
F/A
G
F
E
E
F
3
D.S. AL CODA
(AD LIB. SOLOS ON SECTIONS A & B)
G
F
E
3
CODA
F
REPEAT AD LIB. AS DESIRED
AMAJ7
DMAJ7/A
AMAJ7
DMAJ7/A
AMAJ7
DMAJ13
AMAJ7
DMAJ13
AMAJ7
DMAJ13
AMAJ7
MOLTO RIT.
DMAJ13
A

THE LAMP IS LOW

BALLAD / MEDIUM LATIN

MUSIC BY PETER DEROSE AND BERT SHEFTER
LYRIC BY MITCHELL PARISH

THE LADY SINGS THE BLUES

Lyric by WILLIAM ENGVICK
Music by ALEC WILDER

BLUESY

A
Gm6 Eb7/G Gm6
La - dy sings the blues; she's got them bad, she feels so
Gm7 Gmaj7 Cmaj7 G7 F7 E7
sad. Wants the world to know just what the blues is all a - bout.
Am7 D7(#9) Gm6 Eb7/G Gm6
La - dy sings the blues; she tells her side, noth - ing to
Gm7 Gmaj7 Cmaj7 G7 F7 E7
hide. Now the world will know just what the blues is all a - bout.
Am7 D7(#9) B G Fmaj7 Eb7(b9) G7
The blues ain't noth - in' but a pain in your heart, when you

get a bad start, when you and your man have to part.
A7
I ain't gon-na just sit a-
round and cry, and now I know I won't die be-cause I love him.
D9
C
GM6
Eb7/G
GM6
GM7
La - dy sings the blues; she's got 'em bad, she feels so sad. But
GMAJ7
CMAJ7
G7
F7
D7(#9)
now the world will know. She's nev - er gon - na sing them no more.
1
GM7
D7(#9)
2
GM7
D7(#5)
GM(MAJ7)
No more.

LAURA

Lyric by JOHNNY MERCER
Music by DAVID RAKSIN

FREELY

FMAJ9 C11 FMAJ9 FM7
hall. The laugh
Bb11 Bb7(b9) EbMAJ7 CM7
— that floats on a sum - mer night, that you can
AM7(b5) D7(b9 b5) D9 BM7 E7(#9 #5)
nev - er quite re - call. And you see
8
AM9 D7(b9) GMAJ7 AM7/D
Lau - ra on the train that is pass - ing thru.
GMAJ7 GM9 C7(b9)
— Those eyes, how fa - mil - iar they
FMAJ9 C11 FMAJ9 FM7 FM7/Eb DM7(b5) G7(b9)
seem. She gave your ver - y first
(EbM7 DM7)
CMAJ9 AM11 D13(#11) D7(b9) D13(b9) Ab9 G7(#5) G7
kiss to you. That was Lau - ra, but she's on - ly a
1
C BM7(b5) E7(#9)
dream.
2
C G11 C
dream.

LAZY BIRD

BY JOHN COLTRANE

BRIGHT

A
AM7 D7 CM7 F7 FM11 Bb7
EbMAJ7 AM7 D7 GMAJ7 (AbM7(b5) Db7(b9))
AM7 D7 CM7 F7 FM11 Bb7
EbMAJ7 AM7 D7 GMAJ7
B
BM7 E7 AMAJ7 BbM7 Eb7
AM7 D7 GMAJ7 AbM7 Db7
C
AM7 D7 CM7 F7 FM11 Bb7
EbMAJ7 AM7 D7 1 GMAJ7
2 BM7(b5) E7(b9) AM7(b5) D7(b9) GMAJ7 C7(b9)
FMAJ7 Bb7(b9) A7(b9 b5) AbMAJ7 Db9(#11)
RIT.

LESTER LEAPS IN

UP-TEMPO SWING

WORDS & MUSIC BY LESTER YOUNG

LIL' DARLIN'

WORDS & MUSIC BY NEAL HEFTI

SLOW AND RHYTHMIC
A
B
C
D
(G9 Dm7 Db7(#11))
G9 C7sus C7(b9) FMAJ7 AM7(b5) D7
(AM7 D7(b9))
F13 F7(#5)
(A6)
Bb6 BbM6 F6 F9
AM7(b5) D7(b9 b5)
Gm7 C9 AM7
FMAJ7
F6 AM7 D7(b9 #5)
F6 Ebm11 Ab13 DbMAJ9 GbMAJ9 C9SUS FMAJ7

LIMEHOUSE BLUES

WORDS BY DOUGLAS FURBER
MUSIC BY PHILIP BRAHAM

MED/BRIGHT
London
Limehouse
A
Db9
Oh! Lime-house kid, Oh! Oh! Oh! Lime-house kid,
Bb9
go-ing the way that the rest of them did.
Ab C7 (Edim7) Fm7
Poor bro-ken blos-som and no-bod-y's child,
Bb7 Eb7
haunt-ing and taunt-ing, you're just kind o' wild. Oh! Oh!
B
Db9 Bb7
Oh! Lime-house blues, I've the real Lime-house blues. Can't seem to shake off those
Ab F7 Bbm7 Bbm7(b5)
sad Chi-na blues. Rings on your fin-gers and tears for your crown, that is the sto-
Eb7 Ab Eb7 D7
1
2
-ry of old Chi-na-town.

LINUS AND LUCY

MUSIC BY VINCE GUARALDI

BRIGHTLY
A
Ab
Cb
Ab
1
2
B
Db
Ebsus
N.C.
OPT. 8VA
Db
Ebsus
N.C.
SIMILE

Db Ebsus N.C.
Ab
C
Ab
(L.H./Bass pattern continues)
Cb
Ab
To Coda
Cb
Ab
D
Latin 1st time, swing 2nd time
Eb
Db
C
Db
Solo ad lib
Eb
Db
C
Db
D
Eb
Eb
D.S. al Coda
Coda
Ab
N.C.
Ab
Repeat ad lib. and fade

LITTLE AFRICAN FLOWER

MEDIUM LATIN

BY DUKE ELLINGTON

C
G♭MAJ7
G♭7
C♭7
G♭MAJ7
G♭7(♯11)
A♭7
G♭M7
E♭M7
D7
B♭7
E♭M7
D
A♭M7
G♭M7
E♭M7
B♭M7
E♭M7

Billie Holiday
Courtesy of Star File, Inc.

LOVER MAN
(OH, WHERE CAN YOU BE?)

WORDS AND MUSIC BY JIMMY DAVIS,
ROGER "RAM" RAMIREZ AND JIMMY SHERMAN

SLOW AND BLUESY

AM7 D7 AM7 D7 DM7 G7 DM7 G7
I don't know why but I'm feel-ing so sad,__ I long to try some-thing I've nev-er had,__
The night is cold and I'm so all a-lone__ I'd give my soul just to call you my own__
C7(#9) F7 Ab7 G7 C6/9 BM7(b5) E7(b9)
nev-er had no kiss-in' oh what I've been miss-in' lov-er man, oh, where can you be?
got a moon a-bove me but no-one to love me lov-er man, oh, where can you be?
A
EM7 A7 DMAJ7 C7(#11) BM7 EM7 A13
I've heard it said that the thrill of ro-mance can be like a heav-en-ly dream;
DM7 DM7(b5) G7 CMAJ7 Bb7(#11) BM7(b5) E7(b9)
I go to bed with a pray'r that you'll make love to me strange as it seems.
B
AM7 D7 AM7 D7 DM7 G7 DM7 G7
Some day we'll meet and you'll dry all my tears__ and whis-per sweet lit-tle things in my ears.__
C7(#9) F7 Ab7 G7 C6/9 (BM7(b5) E7(b9))
Hug-gin' and a kiss-in', oh, what I've been miss-in'; lov-er man, oh, where can you be?

LITTLE BOAT

MEDIUM BOSSA

LYRIC BY RONALDO BOSCOLI AND BUDDY KAYE
MUSIC BY ROBERTO MENESCAL

MAIDEN VOYAGE

BY HERBIE HANCOCK

MEDIUM TEMPO, STRAIGHT 8THS

LULLABY OF BIRDLAND

MEDIUM SWING

MUSIC BY GEORGE SHEARING
WORDS BY GEORGE DAVID WEISS

A
EM C#M7(b5) F#7(b9) B7(b9) EM7 CMAJ7
Lul - la - by of bird-land, that's what I always hear,
AM7 D7 (GMAJ7) BM7 EM7 AM7 D7(b9)
when you sigh. Nev - er in my word-land could there be ways to re - veal
G C9 F#M7(b5) B7 EM C#M7(b5)
in a phrase how I feel. Have you ev - er heard two
F#7(b9) B7(b9) EM7 CMAJ7 AM7 D7
tur - tle doves bill and coo when they love?
(GMAJ7) BM7 EM7 AM7 D7(b9) GMAJ7 D7
That's the kind of mag - ic mu - sic we make with our lips when we kiss.

B
C
Gmaj7
E9 E7(♭9) Am Am7
And there's a weep - y old wil - low;
D9 D7(♭9) Gmaj7 E9 E7(♭9)
he real - ly knows how to cry. That's how I'd cry on my pil -
Am Am7 D9 D7(♭9) G B7(♭9)
low, if you should tell me fare - well and good - bye.
Em C♯m7(♭5) F♯7(♭9) B7(♭9) Em7 Cmaj7
Lul - la - by of bird-land, whis - per low, kiss me sweet,
Am7 D7 (Gmaj7) Bm7 Em7 Am7 D7(♭9)
and we'll go fly - in' high in bird-land, high in the sky up a - bove
1 2
Gmaj7 C9 F♯m7(♭5) B7 Gmaj7 Am7 D7(♭9) G6/9
all be - cause we're in love. all be - cause we're in love.

LUSH LIFE

BY BILLY STRAYHORN

BALLAD
(FREELY)
VERSE:
A
B
DbMAJ7 Ab11 Db (BMAJ7) B7
I used to vis - it all the ver - y
DbMAJ7 (BMAJ7) B7 DbMAJ7 (BMAJ7) DbMAJ7 EbM7 (FM7) EMAJ7 F#M7
gay plac - es, those come what may plac - es where one re - lax - es on the ax - is of the
(AbM7 D9(#11) AM9 D9 FM7 D9(#11)) Db6/9 D9 Db6/9 (D9(#11)) D9 Db (BMAJ7) B7
wheel of life to get the feel of life from jazz and cock - tails. The girls I knew had sad and sul - len
DbMAJ7 (BMAJ7) B7 DbMAJ9 (BMAJ7) B7 DbMAJ7 EbM7 (FM7) EMAJ7 F#M7
gray fac - es with dis - tant gay trac - es that used to be there. You could see where they'd been
(AbM9 AM9 D7(#11)) D9-13 Db6/9 D7(#11) Db6/9 GM7(b5) C7
washed a - way by too man - y thru the day, twelve o - clock tales. Then
FM FM6 FM FM6 FM GM7(b5) C7(b9)
you came a - long with your si - ren song to tempt me to mad - ness. I
FM FM6 FM7 FM6 FM (C/E) EbM7 Ab13 B7(b5)
thought for a while that your poig - nant smile was tinged with the sad - ness of a great love for me.

(D13(#11))
Bb7(b9) Ebm7 A9(b5) Ebm7/Ab Ab7(b9)
(BALLAD TEMPO)
Ah! Yes, I was wrong, a - gain I was wrong.
C
CHORUS:
Dbmaj7 (D13(#11)) D9 Dbmaj7 (D13(#11)) D9 Db6 F#m7 B13 Emaj7 D13(#11)
Life is lone - ly a - gain and on - ly last year ev'-ry-thing seemed so sure. Now
Dbmaj7 (D13(#11)) D9 Dbmaj7 (D13(#11)) D9 Db6 Db9 C13 Fmaj7 A13
life is aw - ful a - gain, a trough - ful of hearts could on-ly be a bore. A
Abmaj7 Eb7(#9) Abmaj7 Em7 A7 Dmaj7 Dm7 G7 Cmaj7 Ab13
week in Par - is will ease the bite of it; all I care is to smile in spite of it.
D
Dbmaj7 (D13(#11)) D9 Dbmaj7 (D13(#11)) D9 Db6 C7(b5) B13
I'll for - get you I will, while yet you are still burn-ing in-side my
Fm11 Bb13 F#m9 B13 A7(#9) Ab13 Dbmaj9 Gb13
brain. Ro - mance is mush, sti-fling those who strive. I'll live a lush life in
Fm7 Bb13 F#m9 B13 A7(#5) Ab13 Ab7(#9) A7(#9) Bb7(#9) B7(#9)
some small dive, and there I'll be while I rot with the rest of those whose lives are
C7(#9) D13 Dbmaj7 Ab7(#9) A7(#9) Bb7(#9) B7(#9) C7(#9) D13 Dbmaj7
lone - ly too. those whose lives are lone - ly too.

MAKIN' WHOOPEE

Lyrics by GUS KAHN
Music by WALTER DONALDSON

MODERATELY

Am7 D7) D7 G G7 C (F13) Am7(♭5)
rice, the groom is ner - vous, he an-swers twice. It's real - ly
night, he does - n't phone her, he does - n't write. He says he's
G/D (Em7) E♭7 D7 G C6
kill - ing, that he's so will - ing to make whoop-ee!
"bus - y," but she says "Is he?" He's makin' whoop-ee!
G B (Doim7) A♭oim7 Am7
Pic - ture a lit - tle love - nest,
He does - n't make much mon - ey,
Cm6 G (Doim7) A♭oim7
down where the ros - es cling; pic - ture the same sweet
on - ly six thou - sand per. Some judge who thinks he's
Am7 Cm6 G/D D7
love - nest, think what a year can bring. He's wash - ing
fun - ny says, "You'll pay six to her." He says, "Now
C (A♭oim7 G Am7 D7) D7 G G7
dish - es and ba - by clothes, he's so am - bi - tious he e - ven
Judge, sup - pose I fail?" The judge says, "Budge right in - to
(F13) C Am7(♭5) (Em7) G/D E♭7 D7
sews. But don't for - get folks, that's what you get, folks, for mak - in'
jail. You'd bet - ter keep her, I think it's cheap - er than mak - in'
1 G Em7 Am7(♭5) D7 2 G C7 G6/9
whoop - ee! An-oth - er whoop-ee!"

THE MAN I LOVE

Music and Lyrics by
GEORGE GERSHWIN and IRA GERSHWIN

F-9
(G7(#5) C9 F9(#5))
Eb Abmaj7 Gm Bb7 Eb
make him stay. He'll look at me and smile;
(Gm7(b5))
Ebm Bbm C7(#5)
I'll un - der-stand. And in a lit - tle while, he'll take my hand.
Fm7(b5) Bb13 Eb Ab
And though it seems ab - surd, I know we both won't say a
Eb G7(#5) 8 Cm Cm7 D7(b9) G7(#9)
word. May - be I shall meet him Sun - day, may - be
Cm G7(#5) Cm Cm7 D7(b9) G7(#9)
Mon - day, may - be not. Still I'm sure to meet him one day, may - be
(C7(#5) Fm7) F-9 C
Cm7 Gdim7 Ab Bb7 Bb7 Eb Ebm
Tues - day will be my good news day. He'll build a lit - tle home, just meant for two,
(Gm7(b5))
Bbm C7(#5) Fm7(b5)
from which I'll nev - er roam, who would; would you? And so all else a - bove,
1 2
Bb7 Fm7 Bb13 Eb Ab6 Eb Bb7 Eb
I'm wait - ing for the man I love. love.
Db9

MEDITATION

BOSSA NOVA TEMPO

MUSIC BY ANTONIO CARLOS JOBIM
ORIGINAL WORDS BY NEWTON MENDONCA
ENGLISH WORDS BY NORMAN GIMBEL

B
F6/9
Bb9
Yes, I love you so, and that
EM7
EbDIM7
DM7
G9(#5)
for me is all I need to know.
C
C6/9
(F#M7)
B7SUS
B7
I will wait for you 'til the
C6/9
(DM7 EbDIM7 EM7 A7SUS)
EM7
A7(#9/#5)
sun falls from out of the sky for what else can I do?
DM7
FM6
Bb9
I will wait for you, Me - di -
EM7
A7(b9/#5)
DM7
G13(b9)
C6/9
(G7(#9/#5))
ta - ting how sweet life will be when you come back to me.
D
OPTIONAL TAG
F#M7(b5)
B7SUS
BbMAJ7
A7SUS
DM7(b5)
G7(b9)
CMAJ7

MINNIE, THE MOOCHER

MEDIUM SWING

WORDS & MUSIC BY
CAB CALLOWAY AND IRVING MILLS

VERSE:
A
EM
AM
EM
1. Now here's a sto - ry 'bout Min - nie the Mooch - er.
messed a - round wid a bloke named Smoke - y.
B7
EM
B7
EM
She was a low - down hooch - y cooch - er. She was the rough - est,
She loved him though he was a "coke - y." He took her down to
AM
EM
F♯M7(♭5)
EM/G
B7/A
EM/B
B7
EM
tough - est frail, but Min - nie had a heart as big as a whale. Ho de
Chi - na town, and showed her how to kick the gong a - round. Hi de
B
CHORUS:
ho de ho, (ho de ho de ho.) Rah de dah de dah, (rah de
hi de hi, (hi de hi de hi.) Ree de dah de doo, (ree de
dah de dah.) Tee - dle dee de dee, (tee - dle dee de dee.) Ho de
dah de doo.) Bo de dah do dah, (bo de dah do dah.)
1-6
B7
EM
F♯M7(♭5)
EM
B7
ho de ho, (ho de ho de ho.) 2. She

7
EM B7 EM B7 EM F#M7(b5) B7 EM
ho___ de ho.___) Poor Min', poor Min', poor Min'.

Verse 3:
She had a dream 'bout the King of Sweden.
He gave her things that she was needin'.
Gave her a home built of gold and steel;
A platinum car with diamond-studded wheels.
(To Chorus)

Verse 4:
He gave her his town house and racing horses.
Each meal she ate was a dozen courses.
She had a million dollars in nickels and dimes.
And ev-'ry day she counted 'em a million times.
(To Chorus)

Verse 5:
Now Min' and Smokey they started jaggin'.
They got a free ride in a wagon.
She gave him the money to pay her bail.
But he left her flat in the County Jail.
(To Chorus)

Verse 6:
Poor Minnie met Old Deacon Low-down.
He preached to her she ought to slow down.
But Minnie wiggled her jelly roll.
Deacon Low-down hollered, "Oh, save my soul."
(To Chorus)

Verse 7:
They took her where they put the crazies.
Now poor old Min' is kickin' up daisies.
You've heard my story, this ends the song.
She was just a good gal but they done her wrong.
(To Chorus)

MISS OTIS REGRETS

(SHE'S UNABLE TO LUNCH TODAY)

SLOWLY, OR RUBATO THROUGHOUT

WORDS AND MUSIC BY COLE PORTER

8
EbMAJ7 CM7 FM7 Bb7 Eb6
woke up and found that her dream of love was gone,
mob came and got her and dragged her from the jail,
FM7 EbMAJ7 FM7 GM7 C7(#5)
Ma - dam, she ran to the man who had led her so far a -
Ma - dam, they strung her up - on the old wil - low ac - ross the
FM7 Bb7 EbMAJ7
stray. And from un - der her vel - vet
way. And the mo - ment be - fore she
(A7(#11)) (GM7 Bb7SUS)
BbM7 Eb7 AbMAJ7
gown she drew a gun and shot her lov - er
died, she lif - ted up her love - ly head and
(AbM6 GM7 C7(b9))
EbMAJ7 Eb7 Ab6 EbMAJ7 CM7
down, Ma - dam. Miss Ot - is re - grets she's un -
cried, Ma - dam, "Miss Ot - is re - grets she's un -
FM9 Bb9 Eb 1 FM7 Bb7 2 Eb
a - ble to lunch to - day. When the
a - ble to lunch to - day."

MISTER FIVE BY FIVE

BY DON RAYE AND GENE DEPAUL

MEDIUM SWING
Eb6 Eb6/G Ab6 Bb7 Eb6 Eb6/G Ab6 Bb7
Well
A
Eb6 FM7 Bb7 FM7 Bb7 Eb6
twirl my tur-ban man a - live, here comes Mis - ter Five by Five. He's
Ab7 N.C.
one of those big bad bounc - ing boys. Sol - id a -
Bb7 N.C. B Eb6 Eb6/G
voir - du - pois. Mis - ter Five by Five.
Ab7 Bb7 Eb6 Eb6/G Ab7 Bb7
He's five feet tall and he's five feet wide. He don't mea -
Eb6 Eb7/Db Ab/C Bb6 FM7 Bb
sure no more from head to toe than he do from side to side.
Eb6 N.C. Eb6 Eb6/G Ab6 Bb7
Mis - ter Five by Five, got fif - teen
Eb6 Eb6/G Ab6 Bb7 Eb6 Eb7/Db
chins and a line of jive. He's a mel - low old cat, a

FM7/C Bb6 FM7 Bb6 Eb6
real head fat he be Mis - ter Five by Five.
C
G7 C7
That man can real - ly jump it for a fat man.
F9
The on - ly trou - ble is there's no way of know - ing wheth - er he's
3
N.C. FM9 Bb7(b9) N.C.
D
Eb6 Eb6/G
com - ing a - long or go - ing. Mis - ter Five by Five.
Ab6 Bb7 Eb6 Eb6/G Ab6 Bb7
He's slight - ly plump, on the so - lid side, he don't shake
Eb6 Eb7/Db FM7/C Bb7 Bb6 FM7 Bb6
it no more from head to toe that he do from side to side.
Eb6 N.C. Eb6 Eb6/G Ab6 ADIM7
Mis - ter Five, Five by Five. He's five feet
Eb6/Bb ADIM7 Bb7 Eb7 Ab6 Ab6/C
tall and he's five feet wide. Slight - ly plump and he can jump

D♭6 E♭7 A♭6/C B♭6 E♭6 B♭6 E♭6
'cos he's a mel - low old fat and a real head cat.
E
Fm7 B♭6 N.C. E♭6
Mis - ter Five by Five, he's five feet tall and he's five feet wide.
E♭6 E♭7/D♭ Fm7/C B♭6
He does-n't mea-sure no more oh, from his head to his toe than he
Fm7 B♭7 E♭6 B♭7 E♭6 E♭6/G A♭6 B♭7
do from side to side. Mis - ter Five by five feet Five. He's slight-ly
E♭6 E♭6/G A♭6 B♭7 E♭6 E♭7/D♭
plump, on the so - lid side. He does-n't mea-sure no more from
Fm7/C B♭6 Fm7 B♭7 E♭6
head to toe than - 'll he do from side to side. Mis - ter
F
E♭6 E♭6/G A♭6 B♭7 E♭6 E♭6/G A♭6 B♭7
Five, Mis - ter Five, Mis - ter
E♭6 E♭6/G A♭6 Adim7 B♭7 N.C. E♭6
Five he be just lit-tle Mis-ter Five by Five.

MISTY

SLOW/MEDIUM

WORDS BY JOHNNY BURKE
MUSIC BY ERROLL GARNER

MOMENT'S NOTICE

BY JOHN COLTRANE

BbM7 Eb7 AbMAJ7 Db9 G7 C7(#5)
C
AbM7 Db7 GbMAJ7 FM7 Bb7 EM7 A7
FM7 Bb7 EbMAJ7 AbM7 Db7 DM7 G7
EbM7 Ab7 DbMAJ7 DM7(b5) G7 CM7
BbM7 Eb7 AbMAJ7 Db9 G7 C7
FM7 Bb7 Eb/Bb FM/Bb GM/Bb FM/Bb
Eb/Bb FM/Bb GM/Bb FM/Bb 1 Eb 2 Eb7(#9)

LOVE IS HERE TO STAY

Music and Lyrics by
GEORGE GERSHWIN and IRA GERSHWIN

(Bm7(b5) E7)
G13 Gm7/C C7 Eb9(#11) D9 G7
year but ev - er and a day. The ra - di -
(Am7)
C7 D7 Gm7 C7 Fmaj7 Bb Em7(b5) A7
o and the tel - e - phone and the mov - ies that we know may just be
(D7)
Dm G7 Gm7/C C7
pass - ing fan - cies, and in time may go. But, oh my
B
G9 Gm7 C7 F Am7 D7
dear, our love is here to stay; to - geth - er
(Bm7(b5) E7)
G13 Gm7 C7 Eb9(#11) D9 G7
we're go - ing a long, long way. In time the
(Am7)
C7 D7 Gm7 C7 Eb9 D7
Rock - ies may crum - ble, Gib - ral - tar may tum - ble, they're on - ly made of
Bb Bdim7 F/C D7 Gm7 C9
clay, but our love is here to
1. F6 Am7 D7
stay. It's ver - y
2. F6
stay.

MOOD INDIGO

MEDIUM BALLAD

WORDS AND MUSIC BY DUKE ELLINGTON,
IRVING MILLS AND ALBANY BIGARD

MOONLIGHT IN VERMONT

MUSIC BY KARL SUESSDORF
LYRIC BY JOHN BLACKBURN

THE MORE I SEE YOU

WORDS BY MACK GORDON
MUSIC BY HARRY WARREN

MR. LUCKY

MUSIC BY HENRY MANCINI
WORDS BY JAY LIVINGSTON AND RAY EVANS

* MEDIUM
A
D13 Dm9 G13 G7(b9 #5)
They call us luck - y, you and I, luck - y
Cm9 F13 F7(b9 #5) Bbmaj9 Bb6/9 Am9
girl, luck - y guy. When you take my hand or
D9(b5) Bm7 Em7 Cm9 Cm9/Bb Am7 D7
touch my cheek I know I'm on a life - time luck - y
Dm7 G9 A7(#9 #5)
B
D13 Dm9
streak. A luck - y rain - bow lights the sky
G13 G7(b9 #5) Cm9 F13 F7(b9 #5) Bbmaj9 E9(b5)
when we kiss when we sigh.
He: They
She: They
Ebmaj7 D9 D9/C Bm7(b5) E7(b9 #5) Am9
say I'm luck - y, mis - ter luck - y guy and you're the
say you're luck - y, mis - ter luck - y guy but dar - ling,
D9sus G6/9 A7(#9 #5) G6/9
1
2
rea - son why. They call us I.
so am

* ORIGINAL HENRY MANCINI INSTRUMENTAL IN KEY OF C.

MR. PC

BY JOHN COLTRANE

FAST SWING
CM
GM CM FM
CM GM CM
Ab7 G7(#5) 1 CM GM CM
2 CM GM CM
Ab7 G7(#5) CM GM CM6

MY FOOLISH HEART

WORDS BY NED WASHINGTON
MUSIC BY VICTOR YOUNG

MY FUNNY VALENTINE

WORDS BY LORENZ HART
MUSIC BY RICHARD RODGERS

FREELY
VERSE:
CM Bb7 Eb G7
Be - hold the way our fine-feath-ered friend his vir - tue doth pa - rade. Thou
CM Bb7 Eb G7
know - est not, my dim - wit - ted friend, the pic - ture thou hast made. Thy
C7 FM G
va - cant brow and thy tou - sled hair con - ceal thy good in - tent. Thou
CM Bb7 Eb DM7(b5) G7(#5)
no - ble, up - right, truth - ful, sin - cere and slight - ly dop - ey gent, you're:
A
SLOW / MED.
CHORUS:
CM CM(MAJ7) CM7 CM6
My fun - ny val - en - tine, sweet com - ic val - en - tine,
AbMAJ7 FM11 DM7(b5) G7(b9)
You made me smile with my heart.
CM CM(MAJ7) CM7 CM6
Your looks are laugh - a - ble, un - pho - to - graph - a - ble,

(D♭7)
A♭maj7 Gm7 Fm7 A♭m6 B♭11 B♭13(♭9)
yet you're my fav - 'rite work of art. Is your
B
E♭maj7 Fm7 B♭7 E♭ Fm7 B♭7 E♭ Fm7 B♭7 E♭ Fm7 B♭7
fig - ure less than Greek? Is your mouth a lit - tle weak? When you
(A♭7 G7 Cm7 B7 B♭m7 A7)
E♭maj7 G7(♭9 #5) G7(♭9) Cm7 B♭m7 E♭7(♭9) A♭maj7 Dm7(♭5) G7(♭9)
o - pen it to speak, are you smart? But
C
Cm Cm(maj7) Cm7
don't change a hair for me, not if you
Cm6 A♭maj7 Dm7(♭5) G7(♭9)
care for me. Stay, lit - tle Val - en - tine,
Cm7 B7 B♭m11 A7(♭5) A♭maj7 Gm7 C7(♭9) Fm7 B♭7(♭9)
stay. Each day is Val - en - tine's
1. E♭ Dm7(♭5) G7(♭9)
day.
2. E♭ B♭13(♭9) E♭maj7
day.

MY ROMANCE

MUSIC BY RICHARD RODGERS
WORDS BY LORENZ HART

BALLAD OR MEDIUM SWING

MY SHIP

MEDIUM BALLAD

WORDS BY IRA GERSHWIN
MUSIC BY KURT WEILL

MYSTERIOUS TRAVELER

BY WAYNE SHORTER

MODERATE JAZZ-ROCK (SWING 16THS ♫ = ♪³♬)

* SUGGESTED CHORD NAMES

F#7(#9)
N.C.
1
F#7(#9)
2,3
A2

F#m11
4
A2
8
SOLOS:
F#m7
ON CUE:

NAIMA

MEDIUM BALLAD

BY JOHN COLTRANE

A
Bbm9/Eb
Ebm9
(B13(#11)
A13(#11))
Amaj7/Eb
Gmaj7/Eb
Abmaj7
Bbm9/Eb
Ebm9
(B13(#11)
Ab13(#11))
Amaj7/Eb
Gmaj7/Eb
Abmaj7
B
Bmaj7/Bb
Bb13(b9)
Bmaj7/Bb
Bb13(b9)
Dmaj7(#5)/Bb
Bmaj7/Bb
Abmaj7/Bb
(Emaj13(#11))
Eb7sus(b9)/Bb
C
Bbm9/Eb
Ebm9
(B13(#11)
A13(#11))
Amaj7/Eb
Gmaj7/Eb
Abmaj7
Abmaj7
Amaj7/Eb
Gmaj7/Eb
Abmaj7
Amaj7/Eb
Gmaj7/Eb
Abmaj7
Amaj7/Eb
Gmaj7/Eb
Abmaj7
Dbmaj7
Abmaj7
Dbmaj7
Abmaj7
Dbmaj7
Abmaj7

NATURE BOY

Duple on Triple

EASY JAZZ BALLAD/RUBATO

BY EDEN ABBEZ

* ORIGINAL PIANO/VOCAL SHEET MUSIC WAS WRITTEN IN 3/4.

B
Fm11 Bb7(#5) Ebmaj7 Eb6
think of you night and day. Day and night,
E13
Bmaj7 Bb7(#5) Ebmaj7 Eb6
why is it so, that this long -
Bmaj7 Bb7(#5) Ebmaj7 Eb6
ing for you fol - lows wher - ev - er I go? In the
Am7(b5) Abm7 Gm7 Gbdim7
roar - ing traf-fic's boom, in the si - lence of my lone - ly room I
Fm11 Bb7(#5) Ebmaj7 Eb6
think of you, night and day. Night and
C
Gbmaj7 (Emaj13) Ebmaj7
day, un - der the hide of me. There's an
Gbmaj7 (Emaj13) Ebmaj7
oh, such a hun - gry yearn - ing burn - ing in - side of me. And it's
Am7(b5) Abm7 Gm7 Db9 Gbdim7
tor - ment won't be through 'til you let me spend my life mak - ing love to you,
Fm11 Bb7(#5) 1 Eb Cm7 Fm11 Bb13 2 Eb Bb11 Eb
day and night, night and day. Night and day
E13

NIGHT IN TUNISIA

WORDS & MUSIC BY
JOHN GILLESPIE, FRANK PAPARELLI

MEDIUM LATIN / SWING

DM
E♭7
DM
TO CODA
3
EM7(♭5)
A7(♭5)
DM
D
INTERLUDE
EM7(♭5)
E♭7(♯11)
DM
G7(♯11)
GM(MAJ7)
GM7
G♭7(♯9)
FMAJ7
SOLO BREAK:
EM7(♭5)
A7(♭9)
D.S. AL CODA
(WITH REPEATS)
CODA
EM7(♭5)
A7(♭5)
EM7(♭5)
A7(♭5)
EM7(♭5)
A7(♭5)
DM

NIGHT TRAIN

BY JIMMY FORREST, OSCAR WASHINGTON
AND LEWIS SIMPKINS

SLOW-MEDIUM SHUFFLE

OLD DEVIL MOON

WORDS BY E.Y. HARBURG
MUSIC BY BURTON LANE

MODERATE OR BRIGHT

OLEO

BY SONNY ROLLINS

UP-TEMPO SWING
A
Bb6 GM7 CM7 F7 (DM7 G7) Bb6 GM7
CM7 F7 Bb6 Eb6 DM7 GM7
1 CM7 F7
2 CM7 F7 Bb
B
D7 G7
INST. SOLO AD LIB.
C7 F7
C
Bb6 GM7 CM7 F7 (DM7 G7) Bb6 GM7 CM7 F7
Bb6 Eb6 (EDIM7) DM7 GM7 CM7 F7 Bb

ON A CLEAR DAY
(YOU CAN SEE FOREVER)

LYRIC BY ALAN JAY LERNER
MUSIC BY BURTON LANE

MEDIUM SWING

ON GREEN DOLPHIN STREET

MEDIUM LATIN

MUSIC BY BRONISLAU KAPER
LYRICS BY NED WASHINGTON

OUR DELIGHT

MEDIUM SWING

WORDS & MUSIC BY TADD DAMERON

ONE NOTE SAMBA

MUSIC BY ANTONIO CARLOS JOBIM
ORIGINAL WORDS BY NEWTON MENDONCA
ENGLISH WORDS BY JON HENDRICKS

Ab7 Dbmaj7
talk and talk and talk and still say noth - ing, or near - ly noth - ing.
Dbm7 Gb7 Cbmaj7
I have used up all the scale I know and at the end I've come to noth - ing, or sim - ply
C
Cm7(b5) B7(b5) Dm7 Db7
noth - ing. F13 So I come back to this one note as I
Cm7 B7(b5) Dm7
must come back to you, F13 and I'll pour in - to this one
(Gbmaj7 F7(b5))
Db7 Cm7 B7(b5)
note all the love I feel for you. An - y
(Bb7)
Fm7 E7(b5) Ebmaj7
man can sing a sam - ba, an - y fa - so - la - ti - do,
Ab7 Db6 C7
for a man to sing a true note let him sing
1 2
Bmaj7 Bb6 F7(#5) Bmaj7 Bb6
the one he knows. This is the one he knows.

OO-SHOO-BE-DOO-BE

WORDS AND MUSIC BY JOE CARROLL AND BILLY GRAHAM

Db Db7/F Gb7 Ab7(#5) Db Db7/F
shoo - be - doo - be, oo - oo. Oo - shoo-be-doo-be, oo -
C
Gb7 Ab7(#5) Ab13 AbM7
oo. Oo - shoo-be-doo-be, oo - shoo-be-doo-be." Shoo-be-doo-be means that I
Db13 Gb AbM7 Gb/Bb Gb Eb13
love you and oo, that means I love you too. As I pass by I can
D13
hear her say "We'd bet-ter hur-ry and name the day be-cause; Oo -
D
Db Db7/F Gb7 Ab7(#5) Db Db7/F Gb7 Ab7(#5)
shoo-be-doo-be, oo - oo. Oo - shoo-be-doo-be, oo - oo. Oo -
Db Db7/F Gb7 Ab7(#5) Eb13 Ab13 Db
shoo-be-doo-be, oo. Oo - shoo-be - doo be means I love you."

ORNITHOLOGY

BY CHARLIE PARKER

MEDIUM-UP SWING

GM7
C7
FMAJ7
FM7
Bb7
Eb7
AM7(b5)
D7
G
AM7
D7
G/B
Bb7
AM7
Ab7
GMAJ7
1
AM7
D7
2
G

OVER THE RAINBOW

MUSIC BY HAROLD ARLEN
LYRIC BY E.Y. HARBURG

(GM7)
AbMAJ7 Db7 EbMAJ7/Bb C7(b9) F7 Bb7 Eb6 Bb7SUS
8
and the dreams that you dare to dream real-ly do come true. Some
(Eb/Bb
Eb6
FM7/Bb)
FM7 Bb7
day I'll wish up - on a star and wake up where the clouds are far be -
GM11 C7 FM7 Bb7
(Eb/Bb)
Eb6
hind me.
Where trou - bles melt like lem - on drops a -
AM7(b5) D7(b9) GM7 GbDIM7 FM7 Bb9
way, a - bove the chim - ney tops that's where you'll find me.
(AM7(b5) AbM7)
(AM7(b5) D7)
C
Eb6 CM7 GM7 Eb7 AbMAJ7 Bb7SUS GM7 C7-13
Some - where o - ver the rain - bow, blue - birds fly,
(GM7)
Db9
F-7 Bb
13
1
AbMAJ7 Db7 EbMAJ7/Bb C7(b9) F7 Bb7 Eb6 Bb7
E13
birds fly o - ver the rain - bow why then, oh why can't I?
2
(Eb/Bb)
Eb6 Bb7SUS EbMAJ7
I? If hap - py lit - tle blue - birds fly be -
(FM7/Eb
FM7 GM7 AbMAJ7 Bb13(b9))
FM7
Bb9
Eb6/9
yond the rain - bow why oh why can't I?
RIT.

PEG

MEDIUM JAZZ-ROCK

WORDS AND MUSIC BY
WALTER BECKER AND DONALD FAGEN

GMAJ9 F#7(#9) FMAJ9 E7(#9)
Ebmaj9 D7(#9) CMAJ7 G(9)/B CMAJ7 G(9)
I've seen your
A VERSE:
CMAJ7 G(9) CMAJ7 G(9) CMAJ7 G(9) CMAJ7 G(9)
pic - ture, your name in lights a - bove it. This is your
FMAJ7 C(9) FMAJ7 C(9) CMAJ7 G(9) CMAJ7 G(9)
big de - but, it's like a dream come true. So won't you
GMAJ7 D(9) FMAJ7 C(9) CMAJ7 G(9) CMAJ7 G(9)
smile for the cam - 'ra? I know they're gon-na love it. Peg. I like your
CMAJ7 G(9) CMAJ7 G(9) CMAJ7 G(9) CMAJ7 G(9)
pin - shot I keep it with your let-ter. Done up in
FMAJ7 C(9) FMAJ7 C(9) CMAJ7 G(9) CMAJ7 G(9)
blue-print - blue, it sure looks good on you, and when you

GMAJ7 D(9) FMAJ7 C(9) CMAJ7 G(9) CMAJ7 G(9)
smile for the cam - 'ra, I know I'll love you bet-ter.
8
CHORUS:
CMAJ7 G(9)/B A7SUS E7SUS CMAJ7 G(9)/B
Peg, it will come back to you. Peg, it will come
A7SUS E7SUS A/C♯ C G F♯7
back to you. Then the shut-ter falls, you see it
BM7 E7(♯9) AM7 D9SUS TO CODA CMAJ7 G(9)
all in "Three D". It's your fav-'rite for-eign mov-ie.
D.C. AL CODA
CMAJ7 G(9) F♯M7 BM7 EM7 BM7 CMAJ7
CODA CMAJ7 G(9)/B A7SUS E7SUS
mov - ie it will come back to you.
CMAJ7 G(9)/B A7SUS E7SUS A/C♯ C
Peg, it will come back to you Then the shut-ter
REPEAT AND FADE
G F♯7 BM7 E7(♯9) AM7 D9SUS
falls, you see it all in "Three D." It's your fav-'rite for-eign

PERDIDO

WORDS AND MUSIC BY H.J. LENGSFELDER,
ERVIN DRAKE AND JUAN TIZOL

MEDIUM SWING

PRELUDE TO A KISS

BY DUKE ELLINGTON, IRVING MILLS AND IRVING GORDON

BALLAD

PETER GUNN

MEDIUM ROCK

MUSIC BY HENRY MANCINI

C
F9
D
3
3
3
E9/F F9
E9/F F9
E9/F F9
E9/F F9
FM11/Gb
G(9)/F

POINCIANA

WORDS BY BUDDY BERNIER
MUSIC BY NAT SIMON

(Dm7/G
G6 Dm7 G9
some - how I feel the jun - gle heat. With -
Cm7/F)
Cm6 Gmaj9 G6
in me there grows a rhyth - mic sav - age beat.
B (Ebmaj7(♯11)
Gmaj7 G7 Cm Cm6
Love is ev - 'ry where, its mag - ic per - fume fills the
Am7/D Ebmaj7(♯11)
Dmaj7 D6 Cm
air. To and fro you sway, my
Am7/D Ddim7 D13)
Cm6 D7sus D7
heart's in time, I've learned to care. Poin - ci -
C
(Dm7/G
Gmaj9 G6 Dm7
an - a, though skies may turn from blue to gray,
Cm7/F)
G9 Cm6
my love will live for - ev - er and a
1 2
Gmaj9 D13 Gmaj9
day. Poin - ci - day.

POLKA DOTS AND MOONBEAMS

WORDS BY JOHNNY BURKE
MUSIC BY JIMMY VAN HEUSEN

O BALLAD

VERSE:

Dm Db9 F/C Am7 Abm7 Gm7 C9
In my fright-ened arms, pol - ka dots and moon - beams spark-led on a pug - nosed
8
F6 Bm7(b5) E7 Amaj7 A#dim7 Bm7 E7
dream. There were ques - tions in the eyes of oth - er danc - ers
Amaj7 F#m7 Bm7 E7 Amaj7 A#dim7
3
as we float - ed o - ver the floor. There were ques - tions but my
Bm7 E7 A7 D7 Gm7 C7
heart knew all the an - swers, and per - haps a few things more.
C
Fmaj7 Dm7 Gm7 C7 Fmaj7 Dm7
Now in a cot - tage built of li - lacs and laugh - ter I know the mean - ing of the
Gm7 Em7(b5) A7 Dm Db9 F/C Am7 Abm7
words, "Ev - er af - ter." And I'll al - ways see pol - ka dots and moon - beams
Gm7 C9 F6 Gm7 C7(b9) F6/9
1
2
when I kiss the pug - nosed dream. dream.

QUASIMODO

BY CHARLIE PARKER

MEDIUM SWING
A
EbMAJ7
D7
FM7
Bb7
FM7
Bb7
EbMAJ7
G7
CM7
AM7
D7
GM7
C7
F7(b9)
Bb6
CM7
F7
FM7
C7(#5)
FM7
Bb7
B
EbMAJ7

D7 Fm7 Bb7
Fm7 Bb7 Bbm7 F7(#5)
Bbm7 Eb7 Ab6
Dm7 G7 Cm7 Abm6 F7
Eb6 Fm7(b5) Bb7(b9) Ebmaj7
1 Fm7 Bb7
2 Fm7 Bb7 Eb6

QUIET NIGHTS OF QUIET STARS

ENGLISH WORDS BY GENE LEES
ORIGINAL WORDS AND MUSIC BY ANTONIO CARLOS JOBIM

BOSSA NOVA

D7
DM7
and a win-dow look - ing on the moun - tains and the sea.
8
A♭DIM7
D7/A
How love - ly! This is where I want to be.
A♭DIM7
GM7
3
Here, with you so close to me un - til the fin - al
C7SUS
FDIM7
FMAJ7
flick - er of life's em - ber.
(B♭9(♯11) B♭9)
FM7
FM6
EM7
I, who was lost and lone - ly, be - liev - ing life was
AM7
DM7
G7(♭9)
on - ly a bit - ter tra - gic joke, have found with you,
(B♭13)
EM7
A7
DM7
G7
the mean-ing of ex - ist - ence. Oh, my love.
1
C
A7(♯5)
DM9
G13
2
C
G11
CMAJ7

QUIET NOW

LYRIC BY SUZI STERN
MUSIC BY DENNY ZEITLIN

BALLAD

C
AM7 D7 GMAJ7 C13(#11) BM7 Bb7
AbMAJ7 Db7 CM7 B7 AMAJ7 D7
(BM6)
C#M7 CMAJ7 BM11/E E7
D
AM7 FMAJ7 B13(b9) E7(#9) AM7 DM7 G7 CMAJ7 Bb7(#11) A7(#5)
Ab7 G7 E7 AM7 D7(#11) EM7 AM7 DM7 GSUS
EM7 AM7 FMAJ7 BbMAJ7 EM7 EbMAJ7 AbMAJ7 DbMAJ7 CMAJ7

RELAXIN' AT CAMARILLO

BY CHARLIE PARKER

MEDIUM BLUES

CHORD CHANGES FOR SOLOS:

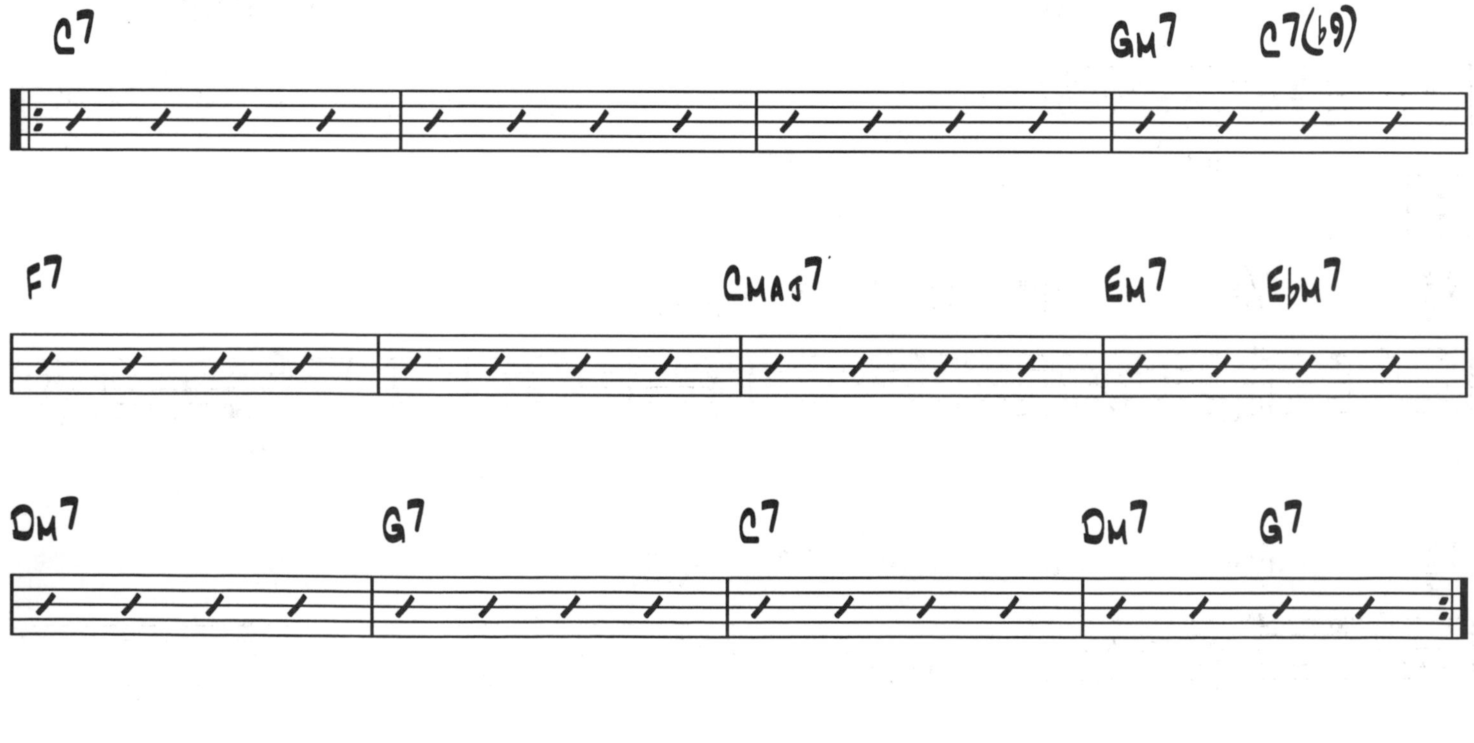

SALT PEANUTS

WORDS AND MUSIC BY
DIZZY GILLESPIE AND KENNY CLARKE

'ROUND MIDNIGHT

WORDS BY BERNIE HANIGHEN
MUSIC BY COOTIE WILLIAMS AND THELONIOUS MONK

BALLAD

1
(Fm7(b5) Bb7(b9))
Cm7(b5) F7(#5) Bb7(#11)
real-ly gets bad 'round mid-night.
2
(Fm7(b5) Bb7(b9))
Cm7(b5) F7(b9) Bb7(b9 #5)
mid - night knows it
Ebmaj7
too. When some
B
Cm7(b5) F7(b9 #5) Bb7(b5)
qua - rel we've had needs mend - ing, does it
Cm7(b5) F7(b9 #5) Bb7(b5)
mean that our love is end-ing?
(Abm7 Db7 Gbmaj7)
Abm7 Fm7 Bb7(#5)
Dar - ling I need you;
Cm7(b5) F7(#5) Bbm7 Eb7 Abm7 Db7 F#m7 B7 Fm7(b5) Bb7(b9)
late - ly I find you're out of my arms and I'm out of my mind.
C
(Ebm Cm7(b5) Fm7(b5) Bb7alt)
Ebm Ebm/D Ebm/Db Cm7(b5) Abm7 Db7
Let our love take wing 'round mid - night, 'round mid - night.
(Ebm7 Ab7)
Cm7 F7(b9) Bm7 E7 Bbm7 Eb7 Abm7 Db7
Let the an-gels sing for your re - turn - ing. Let our love be safe and
(Gbmaj7)
(B9 Bb7(b9))
Ebm7 Ab9 Cm7(b5) F7 Bb7(b9) Ebmaj9
sound when old mid - night comes a - round.

SABIA

MUSIC BY ANTONIO CARLOS JOBIM
PORTUGUESE LYRIC BY CHICO BUARQUE
ENGLISH LYRIC BY NORMAN GIMBEL

MODERATE BOSSA

Bbm7 Eb9sus C7/E Fm E+
some - one's love will speed the night, the lone -
Abm7/Eb Bm6/D C#7 C9(#11) B7sus B7
ly un - want - ed night that may bring me to
Bb9(#11) A9sus A9 Dmaj7/F# F°7
the new day. I'll go back
C
Em7 A7(b9) Dm(maj7) Dm7 Ab°7 Gm7 C7
I know now that I'll go back. They were not in vain,
Fmaj7 F9/C Bbmaj7 Gm7
all the plans I made to de - ceive my - self,
Dm7 F7/C Bbmaj7 Gm7
all the roads I made just to lose my - self,
Dm7 Gm7 Dm7 Gm7 Dm7
all the love I made to for - get my - self, all mis -
Gm7 Dm7 Gm7 Dm7 F°7 Dm7
takes I made just to find my-self. I'll go back,

SATIN DOLL

WORDS AND MUSIC BY JOHNNY MERCER,
DUKE ELLINGTON AND BILLY STRAYHORN

MEDIUM SWING

SCRAPPLE FROM THE APPLE

MEDIUM BOP

BY CHARLIE PARKER

SECRET LOVE

Words by PAUL FRANCIS WEBSTER
Music by SAMMY FAIN

B
(Fm9 Bb13)
EbMaj7 Fm7 Bb7 EbMaj7
So I told a friend - ly star, the
(Eb C7(b9))
Gm7 Ebdim7 Fm7 Bb7
way that dream - ers oft - en do,
Fm7 Bb7 Fm11 Bb13
just how won - der - ful you are and
(Fm6 Bb7 Dm7(b5) G7(b9 #5))
Eb
why I'm so in love with you.
C
Cm7 F7 BbMaj7 BbMaj7 Bb6
Now I shout it from thc high - est hills,
(Db9)
Bbm7 Eb7 AbMaj7 Abm7
e - ven told the gold - en daf - fo - dils. At
D
(Fm7)
Eb Gm7(b5) C7(b9) Fm7
last my heart's an o - pen door, and my se-cret love's no
1 2
Bb7 Eb C7(#9 #5) Fm9 Bb13 Eb Bb11 Eb
se - cret an - y more. more.

SKYLARK

WORDS BY JOHNNY MERCER
MUSIC BY HOAGY CARMICHAEL

SO NICE (SUMMER SAMBA)

BY MARCOS VALLE AND PAULO SERGIO VALLE
(ORIGINAL WORDS AND MUSIC)
AND NORMAN GIMBEL (ENGLISH WORDS)

MEDIUM BOSSA

SOLAR

BY MILES DAVIS

A
MEDIUM SWING
CM(MAJ7)
GM7
C7
FMAJ7
FM7
Bb7
EbMAJ7
EbM7
Ab7
DbMAJ7
DM7(b5)
G7(b9)
B
CM(MAJ7)
GM7
C7
FMAJ7
FM7
Bb7
1
REPEAT FOR SOLOS
EbMAJ7
EbM7
Ab7
DbMAJ7
DM7(b5)
G7(b9)
2
DM7(b5)
G7(b9)
CM(MAJ7)

SOLITUDE

LYRIC BY EDDIE DE LANGE & IRVING MILLS
MUSIC BY DUKE ELLINGTON

SOME OTHER BLUES

BY JOHN COLTRANE

MEDIUM-UP SWING
A
F7
Bb9sus
F7
B7
Bb7
Eb7
Ab7
Db7
1
C13
Bb13/C
F7
2
C13
Bb13/C
F7
B
CHORD CHANGES FOR SOLOS:
F7
Bb7
F7
Bb7
F7
C7
F7
C7

SPRING CAN REALLY HANG YOU UP THE MOST

BALLAD
VERSE:

LYRICS BY FRAN LANDESMAN
MUSIC BY TOMMY WOLF

CMAJ7 B♭MAJ7 CMAJ7 B♭MAJ7 CMAJ7 B♭MAJ7
most. Morn - ing's kiss wakes trees and flow - ers
most. Col - lege boys are writ - ing son - nets;
CMAJ7 AM7 DM7 G7 EM7 A7(♭9)
and to them I'd like to drink a toast; I
in the "ten - der pas - sion" they're en - grossed. But
F♯M7(♭5) FM7 C/E D7
walk in the park just to kill lone - ly hours.
I'm on the shelf with last year's eas - ter bon - nets.
B
DM7 G7 CMAJ7 GM7 CMAJ7
Spring can real - ly hang you up the most. All aft - er - noon those
Spring can real - ly hang you up the most. Love came my way I
GM7 CMAJ7 GM7 CMAJ7 GM7 CMAJ7
birds twit - ter twit. I know the tune, "This is love this is it."
hoped it would last. We had our day, now that's all in the past.
CM7 FMAJ7 CM7 FMAJ7 F♯M7 B7 EMAJ7
3 3
Heard it be - fore and I know the score; and I've de - ci - ded that
Spring came a - long a sea - son of song; full of sweet prom - ise, but
C
AM7 D7 GMAJ7 FMAJ7 CMAJ7 B♭MAJ7
3
Spring is a bore. Love seemed sure a - round the New Year,
some - thing went wrong. Doc - tors once pre - scribed a ton - ic,

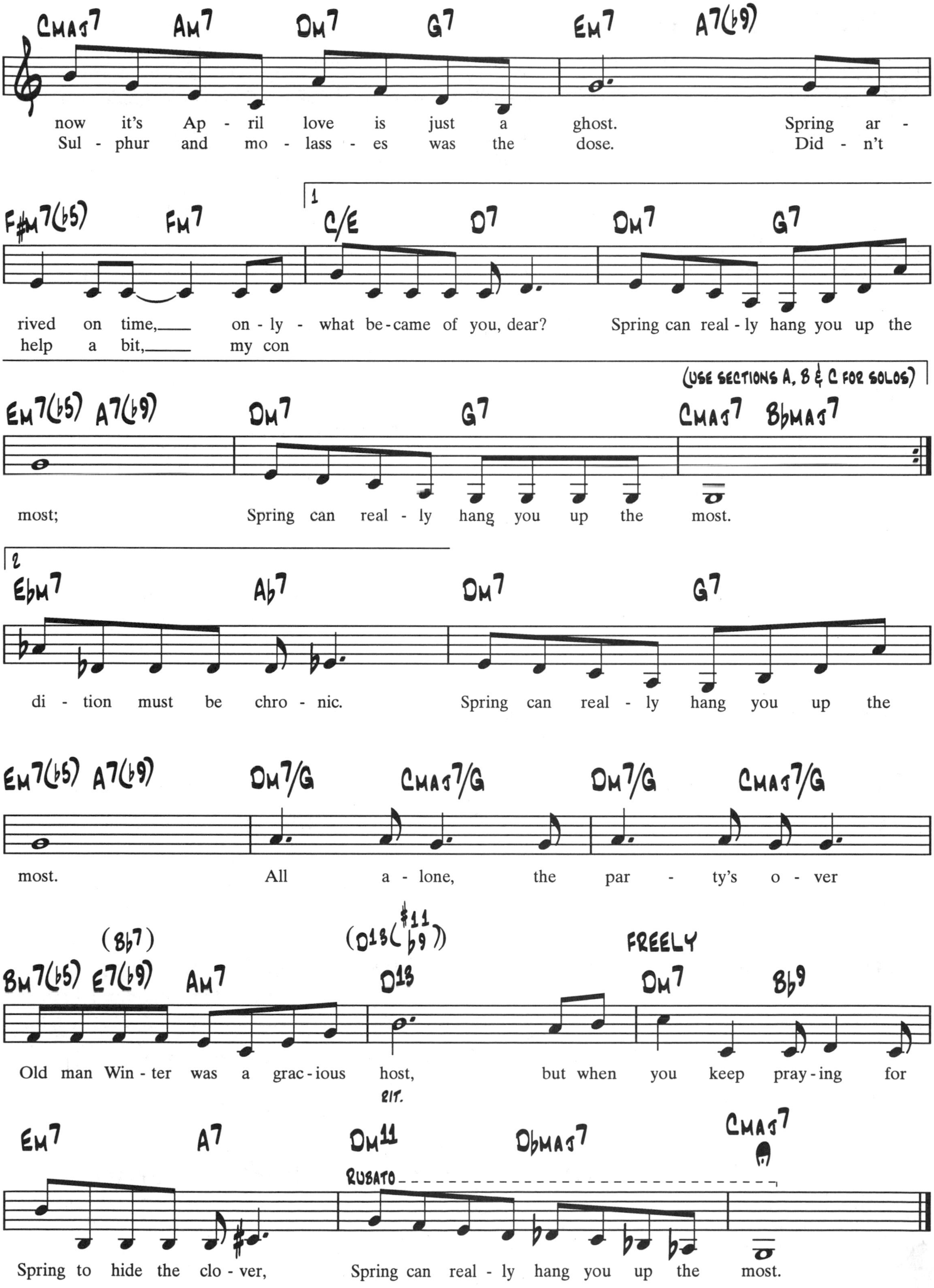
CMAJ7 AM7 DM7 G7 EM7 A7(b9)
now it's Ap - ril love is just a ghost. Spring ar -
Sul - phur and mo - lass - es was the dose. Did - n't
F#M7(b5) FM7
rived on time, on - ly -
help a bit, my con
1
C/E D7 DM7 G7
what be-came of you, dear? Spring can real - ly hang you up the
EM7(b5) A7(b9) DM7 G7 CMAJ7 BbMAJ7
most; Spring can real - ly hang you up the most.
(USE SECTIONS A, B & C FOR SOLOS)
2
EbM7 Ab7 DM7 G7
di - tion must be chro - nic. Spring can real - ly hang you up the
EM7(b5) A7(b9) DM7/G CMAJ7/G DM7/G CMAJ7/G
most. All a - lone, the par - ty's o - ver
(Bb7) (D13(#11 b9))
BM7(b5) E7(b9) AM7 D13
FREELY
DM7 Bb9
Old man Win - ter was a grac - ious host, but when you keep pray - ing for
RIT.
EM7 A7 DM11 DbMAJ7 CMAJ7
RUBATO
Spring to hide the clo - ver, Spring can real - ly hang you up the most.

SOME OTHER TIME

WORDS BY BETTY COMDEN AND ADOLPH GREEN
MUSIC BY LEONARD BERNSTEIN

we'll catch up some oth - er time.
B
Just when the fun is start - ing, comes the time for
part - ing. But let's be glad for what we've had and
what's to come.
C
There's so much more em - brac - ing
still to be done, but time is rac - ing. Oh, well, we'll catch up some
1
oth - er time.
2
oth - er time.

SOMEONE TO WATCH OVER ME

MUSIC AND LYRICS BY
GEORGE GERSHWIN AND IRA GERSHWIN

(G7(♯5) C9 FM7)
FM7 C7/G A♭6 AM7(♭5) B♭7SUS B♭7 E♭ G7(♯5) A♭MAJ7 B♭7
some - one who'll watch o - ver me.
(F7/A)
E♭ E♭13 A♭6 A♭DIM7 E♭/G F♯DIM7 B♭7/F EDIM7
I'm a lit - tle lamb who's lost in the wood. I know I could al - ways be good
FM7 C7/G A♭6 AM7(♭5) B♭7SUS B♭7 E♭ E♭7 A♭ B♭9 E♭ E♭7
to one who'll watch o - ver me. Al - though he
B
A♭ E♭/G
may not be the man some girls think of as hand - some, to
(AM7(♭5) D7)
D7 G7 C C7 F9 B♭7
my heart, he car - ries the key.
C
(F7/A)
E♭ E♭13 A♭6 A♭DIM7 E♭/G F♯DIM7
Won't you tell him, please, to put on some speed, fol - low my lead.
B♭7/F EDIM7 FM7 C7/G A♭6 AM7(♭5) B♭7SUS B♭7
Oh, how I need some - one to watch o - ver
1
E♭ E♭7 A♭ G7(♯5) FM9 B♭7(♯5)
me.
2
E♭ E♭7 A♭ A♭M E♭
me.

THE SONG IS YOU

MUSIC BY JEROME KERN
LYRICS BY OSCAR HAMMERSTEIN II

C
Emaj7 F#m7 B7
I a - lone have heard this love - ly strain.
*(Bbm7(b5) Eb7)
Emaj7 A#m7(b5) D#7
I a - lone have heard this glad re - frain.
G#m7 C#9
Must it be for - ev - er in - side of me. Why can't I
F#13 B13
let it go, why can't I let you know. Why can't I
D
Cmaj7 Ebdim7 Dm7 G7
let you know the song my heart would sing? That beau - ti - ful
Cmaj7 Gm7 C13 Fmaj7 Bb13
rhap - so - dy of love and youth and spring. The mu - sic is
Em7 A7 Dm7 G13
sweet, the words are true. The song is
1
C F7 Em7 Dm11 G13
you.
2
C G11 C Cmaj7
you.

* ENHARMONIC CHORD LABELING.

SOPHISTICATED LADY

Words and Music by DUKE ELLINGTON, IRVING MILLS and MITCHELL PARISH

B
(Bm7 E7(b9))
Gmaj7 Em7 Am7 D7 G7 Gdim7
Db7
Smok - ing, drink - ing, nev - er think - ing of to - mor - row,
Am7 D7(b9) Gmaj7 Em7 Am7 D7
non - cha - lant, dia - monds shin - ing danc - ing, din - ing with some
(Bbm7 Cm7(b5) F7(b9))
Gmaj7 Bdim7 Cm7 Eb7 D7
Db7
man in a res - tau - rant, is that all you real - ly want?
C
(C7(b5) Bb7(b5)) (Abdim7 Abmaj7)
Bbm Bbm7 Gb7 F7 E7 Eb7 Abmaj7
No, soph - is - ti - cat - ed la - dy, I know you miss the
(D7(b5)) (C7(b5))
Ab7 G7 Gb7 F7 Bb7 Bbm7 Eb13
3
love you lost long a - go. And when no - bo - dy is nigh, you
1
Ab6 Cm7(b5) F7(#9) F7(b9)
2
Ab6
cry. They cry.

SPAIN

BRIGHT LATIN

BY CHICK COREA

A
N.C.
EM11
F#SUS
F#
B
G
C
F#7
EM7
A7
DMAJ7
(GMAJ7)
C#7
F#7(b9)
BSUS
B
D
N.C.
TO CODA

* SOLO ON E. AFTER EACH SOLO, REPEAT MELODY AT E (USE CUE NOTES) THEN D.S. 𝄋 AL 2ND ENDING. AFTER LAST SOLO, D.C. AL CODA.

SPEAK LOW

WORDS BY OGDEN NASH
MUSIC BY KURT WEILL

LATIN OR SWING
A
GM9 (C13 C9) GM9 (C13 C9)
Speak low when you speak, love. Our sum-mer
GM9 C9 (C13 GM9 C9 AM11) F6 D7
day with-ers a-way too soon, too soon. Speak
BbM9 (Eb13 Eb9) BbM9 (Eb13 Eb9)
low, when you speak, love. Our mo-ment is
DM7 G13 GM7/C C7(b9) F6 AM7 D7
swift, like ships a-drift, we're swept a-part too soon. Speak
B
GM9 (C13 C9) GM9 (C13 C9)
low dar-ling, speak low. Love is a
GM9 C9 (C13 GM9 C9 AM11) F6 D7
spark lost in the dark too soon, too soon. I
BbM9 (Eb13 Eb9) BbM9 (Eb13 Eb9)
feel wher-ev-er I go that to-mor-row is

Dm7 G13 Gm7/C C7(b9) F6
near, to-mor-row is here and al-ways too soon.
C
Fm7 Db7(#11)
Time is so old and love so brief.
EbMaj7 Db7 C7
Love is pure gold and time a thief. We're
D
Gm9 (C13 C9) Gm9 (C13 C9)
late darling, we're late. The cur-tain de-
Gm9 C9 (C13 Gm9 C9 Am11) F6
seconds, ev-'ry-thing ends too soon, too
D7-13 Bbm9 (Eb13 Eb9) Am7
soon. I wait, dar-ling, I wait.
D7(b9) G9 C7(#5)
Will you speak low to me, speak love to me and
1 F6 Gm7 C7(#5)
soon. Speak
2 F
soon.

ST. THOMAS

MEDIUM CALYPSO

BY SONNY ROLLINS

A
C6/9 (F7) EM7 A7 DM7 G7 C6
(G7 C6 F7) EM7 A7 DM7 G7 C6
EM7(b5) A7(b9) DM7 G7
C6 C9/E F6 F#DIM7 C/G G7 C6
B SOLOS
C6 (F7 EM7 A7) A7 DM7 G7 C6 (G7)
(C6 F7 EM7 A7) A7 DM7 G7 C6
EM7(b5) A7 DM7 G7
C6 C9/E F6 F#DIM7 C/G G7 C6 (G7)

STOMPIN' AT THE SAVOY

MUSIC BY BENNY GOODMAN,
CHICK WEBB AND EDGAR SAMPSON
LYRIC BY ANDY RAZAF

MEDIUM SWING

A

STAIRWAY TO THE STARS

MUSIC BY MATT MALNECK AND FRANK SIGNORELLI
LYRIC BY MITCHELL PARISH

BALLAD
A
C6/9 G7 GM11 C13(b9) FMAJ7
Let's build a stair-way to the stars, and climb that
FM9 Bb7(#11) AM7 D7
stair - way to the stars with love be - side us to
DM11 G7 CMAJ7 A7(b9) Ab9 G7
fill the night with a song.
C6/9 G7 GM11 C13(b9) FMAJ7
We'll hear the sound of vi - o - lins out yon - der
FM9 Bb7(#11) AM7 D7
where the blue be - gins. The moon will guide us as
DM11 G7 C6/9 F7 F#M7(b5) B7(b9)
we go drift - ing a - long.

B
EM7 (F9(#11)) A7 (EM7) AM7 (B7sus(b9))
Can't we sail a - way on a la - zy dai - sy pet - al
EM7 B7(#9) EM7 A7(b9) DM7 (Eb7(#11))
o - ver the rim of the hill? Can't we sail a - way
G9 (DM7 GM7 A7sus(b9)) DM7 D7 DM7 G7(b9)
on a lit - tle dream and set - tle high on the crest of the hill?
C
C6/9 G7 GM11 C13(b9) FMAJ7 (F#M7(b5))
Let's build a stair - way to the stars, a love - ly
FM9 (Bb13) Bb7(#11) AM7 D7 DM11 G7
stair - way to the stars. It would be heav - en to climb to heav - en with
1
C6/9 AM7 D7 G7
you.
2
C6 FM6 C6/9
you.

STAR EYES

WORDS & MUSIC BY
DON RAYE AND GENE DEPAUL

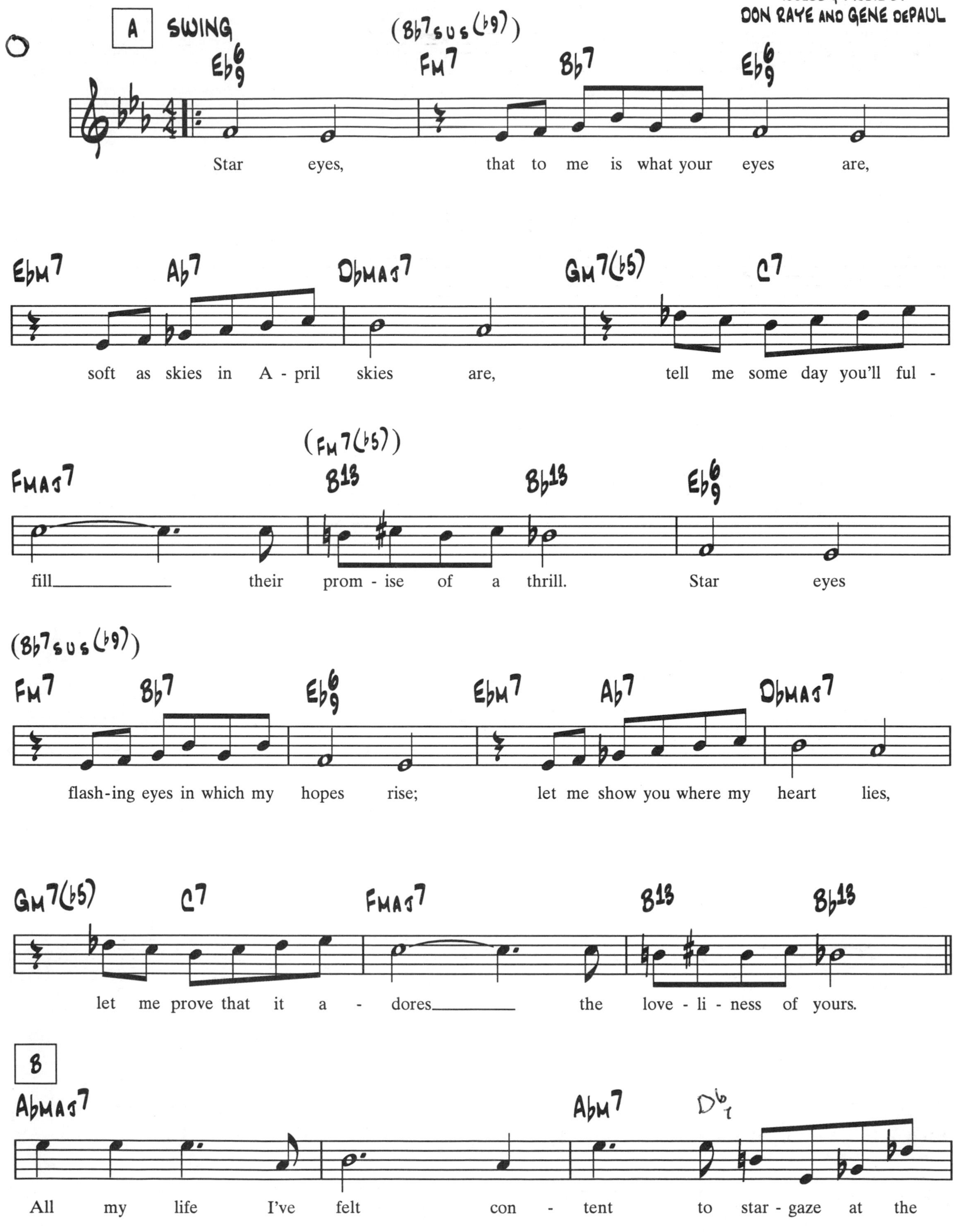
A
SWING
(Bb7sus(b9))
Eb6/9 Fm7 Bb7 Eb6/9
Star eyes, that to me is what your eyes are,
Ebm7 Ab7 Dbmaj7 Gm7(b5) C7
soft as skies in A - pril skies are, tell me some day you'll ful -
(Fm7(b5))
Fmaj7 B13 Bb13 Eb6/9
fill their prom - ise of a thrill. Star eyes
(Bb7sus(b9))
Fm7 Bb7 Eb6/9 Ebm7 Ab7 Dbmaj7
flash-ing eyes in which my hopes rise; let me show you where my heart lies,
Gm7(b5) C7 Fmaj7 B13 Bb13
let me prove that it a - dores the love - li - ness of yours.
B
Abmaj7 Abm7 Db7
All my life I've felt con - tent to star - gaze at the

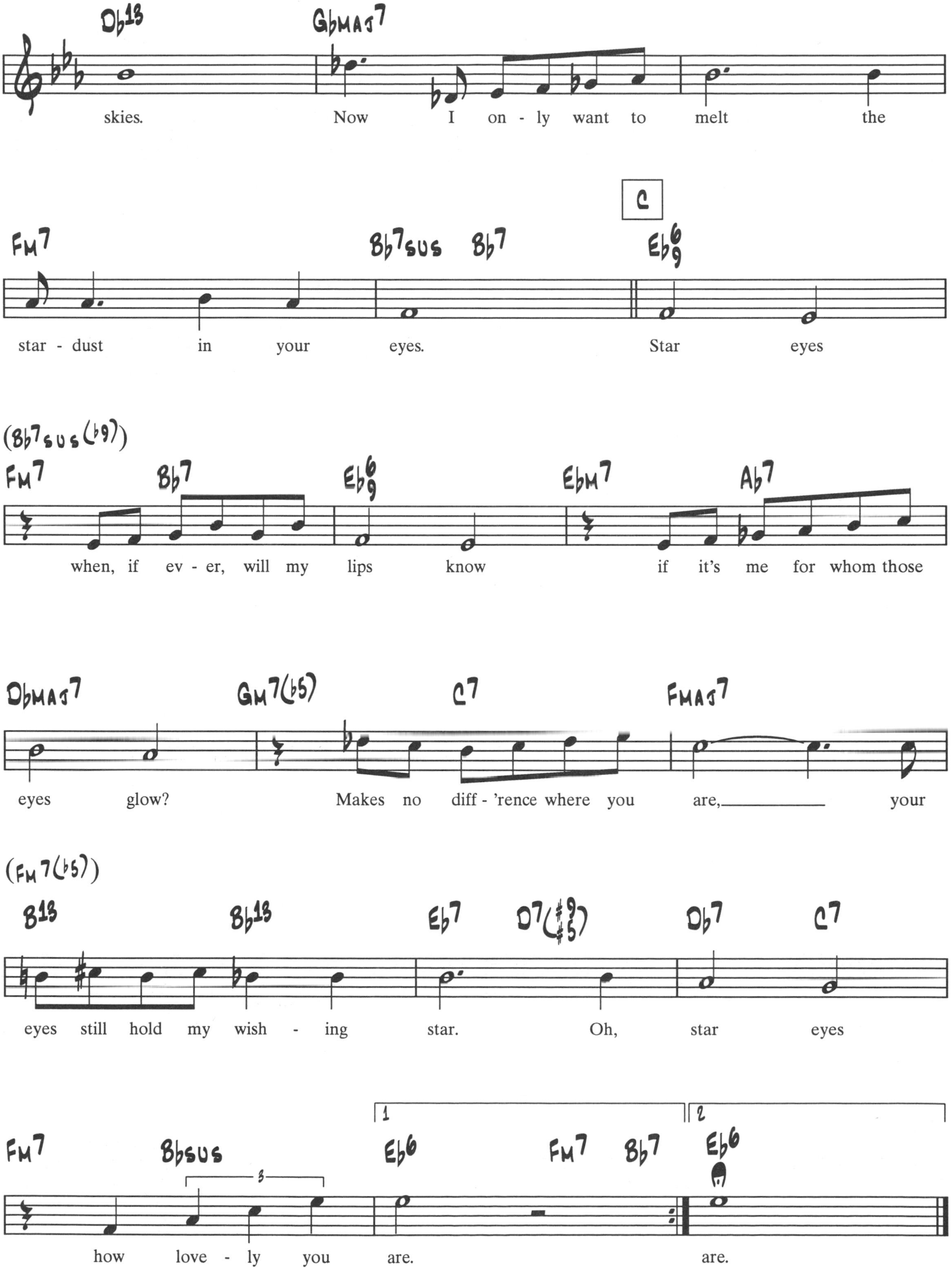
Db13 GbMAJ7
skies. Now I on - ly want to melt the
C
FM7 Bb7SUS Bb7 Eb6/9
star - dust in your eyes. Star eyes
(Bb7SUS(b9))
FM7 Bb7 Eb6/9 EbM7 Ab7
when, if ev - er, will my lips know if it's me for whom those
DbMAJ7 GM7(b5) C7 FMAJ7
eyes glow? Makes no diff - 'rence where you are, your
(FM7(b5))
B13 Bb13 Eb7 D7(#9/#5) Db7 C7
eyes still hold my wish - ing star. Oh, star eyes
1 2
FM7 BbSUS Eb6 FM7 Bb7 Eb6
how love - ly you are. are.

STAR DUST

MUSIC BY HOAGY CARMICHAEL
WORDS BY MITCHELL PARISH

FREELY
VERSE:
CMAJ7 F7(#11) E7(b9) A7
And now the pur-ple dusk of twi-light time steals a-cross the mea-dows of my heart.
DM7 G9 EM7 AM7 F#M7 B7 DM11 G13
High up in the sky the lit - tle stars climb, al - ways re-mind-ing me that we're a - part.
CMAJ7 F7(#11) E7(b9) A7
You wan-dered down the lane and far a-way leav-ing me a song that will not die.
DM7 G9 EM7 AM7 DM7 G7 C
Love is now the star-dust of yes-ter-day, the mu-sic of the years gone by. Some-times I
MED. BALLAD
A
CHORUS:
FMAJ7 FM(MAJ7) FM6 Bb7 CMAJ7
won - der why I spend the lone - ly night dream-ing of a song. The mel - o - dy

Em7 A9 Dm7 A7 Dm7
haunts my rev - er - ie, and I am once a - gain with you, when our
(Cmaj7 Dm7 D#dim7 Em7 Am7)
G13 Dm7 G7 C6
love was new, and each kiss an in - spir - a - tion. But
(G13 C7)
D9 Am9 D7 G7 Dm7 G7 Gdim7 G7 C7(#5)
that was long a - go, now my con - so - la - tion is in the star-dust of a song. Be
8
(C6 Dm7 D#dim7 C/E)
Fmaj7 Fm(maj7) Fm6 Bb7 Cmaj7
side a gar - den wall, when stars are bright, you are in my arms. The night - in - gale
Em7 A9 Dm7 A7 Dm7 Fm7
tells his fair - y tale of par - a - dise where ros - es grew. Though I dream in vain,
(C6 G/B Am7 C/G F#m11 F13(#11) E9(#5) F6 A13 A7(#5))
Bb13 Cmaj7 Am7 Em7 Dm7
in my heart it will re - main: My star-dust mel - o - dy,
(Dm7 G7)
G7
1
C Gm7 C7
2
C Bbmaj9 Cmaj7
the mem - o - ry of love's re - frain. Some-times I frain.

STRAIGHTEN UP AND FLY RIGHT

MEDIUM SWING

WORDS AND MUSIC BY NAT KING COLE AND IRVING MILLS

BbM7 Eb9 Ab6/9 /Gb
in'? Straight - en up and fly
/F /Eb Db6 (FM7) Ab6/C BbM9 Eb13 Ab6/9
right. Cool down, Pa - pa, don't you blow your top. The
8
C7 (GM7 C7) F7
buz - zard told the mon - key, "You are chok - ing me, re - lease your hold and I will
(CM7 F7) Bb9 (FM7 Bb9)
set you free." The mon - key looked the buz - zard right dead in the eye and said, "Your
Eb13 (Gb6/9 G6/9 Ab6/9)
sto - ry's so touch - ing, it sounds just like a lie."
C
Ab6/9 (Ab7/C /Gb Db6/F Doim7 /Eb Ab/Eb Db6 FM7) Ab6/C
Straight-en up and fly right, straight - en up and stay
BbM7 Eb9 Ab6/9 (Ab7/C /Gb Db6/F Doim7 /Eb
right. Straight-en up and fly right. Cool
Ab/Eb Db6 FM7) Ab6/C BbM9 Eb13 Ab6/9
down, Pa - pa, don't you blow your top.

STREET OF DREAMS

WORDS AND MUSIC BY
SAM M. LEWIS AND VICTOR YOUNG

BALLAD / MEDIUM BOSSA

VERSE:

Ebm6 B7 Bb7(#5) Ebm6
Mid - night, you heav - y lad - en, it's mid - night.
Mid - night, look at the stee - ple, it's mid - night,
B7 Bb7(#5) Ebm Db7
Come on and trade in your old dreams for new, your
un - hap - py peo - ple. It's ring - ing with joy, it's
B7 Bb7 Ebm6 A9(#11)
new dreams for old. I know where they're bought, I
ring - ing with cheer, 'cause yes - ter - day's gone, to -
Bbm7(b5) Eb7 Abm6 Bb7(#5) E9
know where they're sold. Mid - night, you've got to get there at
mor - row is near. Mid - night, the heart is light - er at
Ebm6 B7 Bb7(#5) Ebm Db7
mid - night, and you'll be met there by oth - ers like you,
mid - night, things will be bright - er the mo - ment you find

B7 Bb7 Cm7(b5) B7 Fm11 Bb7
broth - ers as blue, smil - ing on the street of dreams.
more of your kind, smil - ing on the street of dreams.
A
Chorus:
F9 Fm9 Bb7
Love laughs at a king, kings don't mean a
Ebmaj7 Abmaj7 Gm11 C7(#5) F9
thing on the street of dreams. Dreams bro - ken in
Fm9 Bb7 Ebmaj7 Bb7(#5) Bbm11 Eb7
two can be made like new on the street of dreams.
B
Ab6 Db7 Ebmaj7
Gold, sil - ver and gold, all you can hold is in the
Db7 C7(b9) F9 B7(#5)
D♭13
moon - beams. Poor, no - one is poor, long as love is
Fm11 Bb7
E13
1 (Optional D.C.) 2
Eb6 C7(b9) Eb6/9
sure on the street of dreams. dreams.

STRUTTIN' WITH SOME BARBEQUE

BY LILLIAN NOBLES,
LOUIS ARMSTRONG & DON RAYE

SLOWLY

SUMMERTIME

BY GEORGE GERSHWIN,
DUBOSE AND DOROTHY HEYWARD AND IRA GERSHWIN

Sweet Georgia Brown

Words and Music by BEN BERNIE, MACEO PINKARD
and KENNETH CASEY

G7
(D♭7(♭5))
Two left feet but oh so neat__ is Sweet Geor-gia Brown.____
C7
C9
They all sigh and wan-na die__ for Sweet Geor-gia Brown,____ I'll tell__ you just
F
GM7
C7(♯5)
F
EM7(♭5)
A7(♭9)
why,________ you know__ I don't lie, not much!
8
D7
(A♭7(♭5))
It's been said she knocks 'em dead__ when she lands in town.____
All those tips the por - ter slips__ to Sweet Geor - gia Brown,____
G7
A7
DM
Since she came why it's a shame_ how she cools 'em down.____ Fel - lers____
They buy clothes at fash-ion shows_ with one dol - lar down,____ oh, boy,____
EM7(♭5)
A7
DM
EM7(♭5)
A7
F7
E7
she can't get____ are fel - lers____ she ain't met.____ Geor - gia claimed_ her
tip your hats,____ oh, joy,____ she's the 'cats.'____ Who's that, mis - ter?
1
(OPTIONAL D.C.)
2
E♭7
D7
G7
C7
F
A7
F
Geor - gia named__ her
T'ain't her sis - ter,
Sweet Geor-gia Brown____

SWEET LORRAINE

MUSIC BY CLIFF BURWELL
WORDS BY MITCHELL PARISH

MEDIUM SWING

TENOR MADNESS

BY SONNY ROLLINS

FAST SWING

Bb7
Eb7
Bb7
Eb7
Bb7
CM7
F7
Bb7
Bb7
Eb7
Bb7
Eb7
Bb7
CM7
F7
1
Bb7
2
Bb7
Bb13(#11)

T'AIN'T NOBODY'S BIZ-NESS IF I DO

MODERATE BLUES TEMPO

WORDS AND MUSIC BY PORTER GRAINGER AND EVERETT ROBBINS

D7 Gm7 Bb/F Eb7 Edim7
per - se - cute me, I choose that you would shoot me;
church on Sun - day then ca - ba - ret on Mon - day,
Bb F7 Bb Cm7 C#dim7 Bb/D
t'ain't no - bod - y's biz - ness if I do.
Bb6/9 D7 Gm7 Bb/F
If I should get the fee - lin' to dance up -
If a friend ain't got no mon - ey and I say
Eb7 Edim7 Bb F7
on the cei - lin' t'ain't no - bod - y's biz - ness if I do.
"take all mine hon - ey",
Bb G7 C7 F7(#5) Bb6/9
If I let my
If I give her
D7 Gm7 Bb/F Eb7 Edim7
best com - pan - ion drive me right in - to the can - yon,
my last nick - el and it leaves me in a pick - le,
Bb F7
t'ain't no - bod - y's biz - ness if I
1 Bb F7 (OPTIONAL D.C) 2 Bb
do. do.

TAKE FIVE

BY PAUL DESMOND

A
MEDIUM SWING
EbM BbM7 EbM BbM7
EbM BbM7 EbM BbM7 EbM BbM7 EbM BbM7
EbM BbM7 EbM BbM7
B
(FM7(b5))
CbMAJ7 AbM7
BbM7 EbM7 AbM7 Db7 GbMAJ7
(GDIM7)
(FM7(b5))
CbMAJ7 AbM7 BbM7 EbM7 AbM7 Db7
C
FM7(b5) Bb7(b9) EbM BbM7 EbM BbM7

TO CODA
EbM BbM7 EbM BbM7 EbM BbM7
EbM BbM7 EbM BbM7 EbM BbM7
D
CHANGES FOR IMPROVISED SOLOS
REPEAT AD LIB. THEN
D.S. AL CODA
EbM BbM7 EbM BbM7 EbM BbM7 EbM BbM7
CODA
EbM BbM7 EbM BbM7 EbM BbM7
EbM BbM7 EbM BbM7 EbM BbM7
EbM BbM7 EbM BbM7 EbM BbM7
EbM BbM7 EbM BbM7 EbM

TEACH ME TONIGHT

WORDS BY SAMMY CAHN
MUSIC BY GENE DEPAUL

Charles Mingus
Courtesy of Roberto Rabanne, Star File, Inc.

THAT OLD FEELING

WORDS & MUSIC BY
LEW BROWN AND SAMMY FAIN

THIS CAN'T BE LOVE

WORDS BY LORENZ HART
MUSIC BY RICHARD RODGERS

THEY CAN'T TAKE THAT AWAY FROM ME

Music and Lyrics by
GEORGE GERSHWIN and IRA GERSHWIN

(E♭MAJ7 FM7 GM7 C7(♯9 ♯5))
E♭6 E♭MAJ7 E♭/G G♭DIM7 FM7 A♭/B♭
— the way you sing off key, — the way you haunt my dreams, —
B♭M7 E♭7 A♭MAJ7 FM7 B♭7 E13 E♭6 AM7(♭5) D7(♭9)
— no, no! They can't take that a-way from me. — We may
B
GM7 AM7(♭5) D7(♭9) GM7 AM7(♭5) D7(♭9) GM7 EM7(♭5) A7 AM11 D7
nev-er, nev-er meet a-gain on the bump-y road to love. Still I'll
GM7 AM7(♭5) D7(♭9) GM7 C7 F7 A♭/B♭
al-ways, al-ways keep the mem-r'y of the way you hold your knife, —
C
(E♭MAJ7 FM7 GM7 C7(♯9 ♯5))
E♭6 E♭MAJ7 E♭/G G♭DIM7 FM7 A♭/B♭
— the way we danced till three, — the way you've changed my life, —
B♭M7 E♭7 A♭MAJ7 FM7 B♭7
— no, no! They can't take that a-way from me! —
(E♭6 A♭M9 G7(♯5) C7(♭9) F7)
CM FM7(♭5) E♭/B♭ FM7/B♭ B♭13
D♭13 E13
— No, they can't take that a-way from
1 E♭ A♭/B♭ 2 E♭ E♭6
me! The way you wear your hat, — me! —

THIS MASQUERADE

MODERATE LATIN/ROCK

WORDS AND MUSIC BY LEON RUSSELL

DM7 G13 G7(#5)
We tried to talk it ov - er, but the words
CMAJ7 GM7
got in the way. We're lost in - side
G13 G7(#5) C7SUS Gb13
this lone - ly game we play.
C
FM FM(MAJ7) FM7
Thoughts of leav - ing dis - ap - pear ev - 'ry time I see your eyes
Bb13 FM7 Db9
no mat - ter how hard I try.
GM11 C7(#9 #5) FM
To un - der - stand the rea -
FM(MAJ7) FM7 Bb13
sons that we car - ry on this way, we're lost
Db7 C7(#5) FM7
in a mas - quer - ade.
Bb13 FM7 Bb13
REPEAT AD LIB. AND FADE

TIME AFTER TIME

LYRIC BY SAMMY CAHN
MUSIC BY JULE STYNE

FREELY
VERSE:
FMAJ7 G9 (EM7) CMAJ7 AM7 Eb9
What good are words I say to you? They can't con -
DM7 G7 G7(b5) CMAJ7 C6
vey to you what's in my heart. If you could
AM AM/G F#M7(b5) FM6 EM7 EM7/D (C/E) C EM7
hear in - stead the things I've
AM7 D9 (C/E Eb7 DM7 Db9(b5)) G9SUS G7
left un - said!
A
MODERATE SWING
CHORUS:
CMAJ7 AM7 DM7 G7 CMAJ7 (EM7) AM7 DM7 G7
Time af - ter time I tell my - self that I'm so
CMAJ7 (C/B) AM7 BM7(b5) E7(b9)
luck - y to be lov - ing you. So

(B♭13(♯11) A7(♭9))
Am Am/G F♯m7(♭5) B7(♭9) Em7 A7(♭9)
luck - y to be the one you run to see in the
Dm7 Em7(♭5) A7(♭9 ♯5) D9 G9sus G7(♭9)
eve - ning when the day is through. I on - ly
8
(Em7)
Cmaj7 Am7 Dm7 G7 Cmaj7 Am7
know what I know, the pass - ing years will
Dm7 G7 Cmaj7 Gm7 C7
show you've kept my love so young so
Fmaj7 Fm7 C6/G F♯m7(♭5) Fm6
new. And time af - ter time you'll
B♭13
Em7 Am7 D9sus D7 C6/G Am7 Dm7 G7(♭9)
hear me say that I'm so luck - y to be lov - ing
1
C6 Am7(♭9) Dm9 G13
you.
2
C6
you.

* TIMES LIE

BY CHICK COREA AND NEVILLE POTTER

JAZZ WALTZ

*THIS ARRANGEMENTS IS DERIVED FROM COMBINED ELEMENTS FROM THE STAN GETZ RECORDING, "CAPTAIN MARVEL" AND THE JOE FARELL RECORDING, "MOONGERMS".

B
FAST SAMBA ♩ = 𝅗𝅥
A
A11
A
SOLO
C
A
AM
A
ON CUE
ADIM(MAJ7)
Bb/A
F#/A
D/A
N.C.
A
(BM/A
AM
A)
D
N.C.
SOLO
ON CUE
GbMAJ7/Ab
Ab11
C/Ab
Bb/Ab
BbDIM7/Ab
N.C.

E
B♭
B♭11
B♭
SOLO
F
B♭11
ON CUE
G/B♭
F/B♭
E♭6/B♭
B♭
B♭11
B♭
D.S. 𝄋 AL CODA
(TEMPO I)
B♭11
B♭
B♭11
B♭
E9(♯11)
CODA
EM
AM7
C♯M7(♭5)
F6
EM/B
1
F♯7
B
BM7
2
B7(♭9)
EM
AM11
EM
AM11
EM
AM11
E
RIT.

TONES FOR JOAN'S BONES

GENTLE SWING
BY CHICK COREA
A
D6/9 DM9(#5)
D7(b9) F7(b9) Bb6/9 AbM7 Gb6/9 F13 BbM7(b5)
Eb7(#9) AbM7
AbM7/Gb Bb7(b9)/F EMAJ13 B EbMAJ7 GbMAJ7
FMAJ7 AbMAJ7 CMAJ7 EbMAJ7 DbM9 A13(b9)
C
D6/9 DM9(#5) D7(b9)
F7(b9) Bb6/9 (AM7 GM7 F7) EM7 A7 BbDIM7
BM7 E13 EM11 F#M11 FM11 Bb13
EbMAJ9 DM7 CM7 F7(#9) EM7 F#M7 G A7(b9) EbMAJ7(#11)

TUNE UP

Duple on Triple

D Mayor on D Minor

FAST SWING

BY MILES DAVIS

TWISTED

MUSIC BY WARDELL GRAY
LYRIC BY ANNIE ROSS

* VOCAL SUNG ONE OCTAVE LOWER.

CMAJ7 EM7 A7 DM7
What's so strange when you know that you're a wiz-ard at three?
G7 C6 A7(b9) DM7 G7(#5)
C
I knew that this was meant to be. Well I heard
C7 F7 C7
lit - tle child-ren were sup - posed to sleep tight, that's why I drank a fifth of
F7
vod - ka one night. My par-ents got fran - tic did - n't know what to do, but
CMAJ7 EM7 A7(b9) DM7
I saw some cra - zy scenes be - fore I came to. Now, do you think I was cra - zy?
G7 C6 A7 DM7 G7(#5)
D
I may have been on - ly three but I was swing-in'. They all laughed at
C7 F7 C7
A. Gra-ham Bell, they all laughed at Ed - i - son and al - so at Ein - stein, so
F7
why should I feel sor - ry if they just could - n't un - der - stand the

CMAJ7 EM7 EbM7
rea-son-ing and the log-ic that went on in my head? I had a brain, it was in-sane. Sol -
DM7 G7 C6 EbDIM7
diers used to laugh at me when I re-fused to ride on all those dou - ble deck-er bus - es all be -
DM7 G7 C6
cause there was no driv - er on the top. My a - na-lyst
E
C7 F7 C7
told me that I was right out of my head, the way he de - scribed it he said I'd be
but I said, "Dear Doc - tor, I think that it's
C7(b5) F9(#11)
bet - ter dead than live. I did-n't lis - ten to his jive, I
you in - stead. 'Cause I have got a thing that's u - nique and new, it
CMAJ7 EM7 A7 DM7
knew all a - long he was all wrong, and I knew that he thought
proves that I have the last laugh on you. 'Cause in - stead of one head
1
G7 C6 A7(b9) DM7 G7(#5)
I was cra - zy but I'm not, oh, no. My an - a - lyst
2
G7 C6 C7
I got two." And you know two heads are bet - ter than one.

VALSE HOT

JAZZ WALTZ

BY SONNY ROLLINS

INTRO: BbM7 Eb7 AbMAJ7 BbM7 Eb7 AbMAJ7 BbM7 Eb7 AbMAJ7
EbM7 Ab7 DbMAJ7 EbM7 Ab7 DbMAJ7 EbM7 Ab7 DbMAJ7
A
AbMAJ7 DbMAJ7 CM7 F7
BbM7 Eb7 CM7(b5) F7(b9)
BbM7 DbM7 CM7 F7(#5)
BbM7 Eb7
1
AbMAJ7 Eb7
2
AbMAJ7

WATCH WHAT HAPPENS

BOSSA NOVA

MUSIC BY MICHEL LEGRAND
ENGLISH LYRICS BY NORMAN GIMBEL

WATERMELON MAN

BY HERBIE HANCOCK

MEDIUM ROCK

* AS RECORDED BY HERBIE HANCOCK FROM THE RECORDING, "WATERMELON MAN"

WINDOWS

JAZZ WALTZ

BY CHICK COREA

A
BM7
G#M7(b5)
C#7
F#M7
D9SUS
EMAJ7(#11)
B
Ab7
A7
Ab7
A7
Ab7
A7
Ab7
A7
Ab7
C
EMAJ7
D#M7
C#M7
C#M7/B
BbM7(b5)
BbM7(b5)/Ab
Eb7/G
Eb7
AbM
AbM7/Gb
Db7/F
Db7
EMAJ7
D#M7
C#M7
C9(#11)

THE WAY YOU LOOK TONIGHT

WORDS BY DOROTHY FIELDS
MUSIC BY JEROME KERN

MEDIUM OR FAST

GbMAJ7 G°M7 AbM7 Db7
And the laugh that wrin - kles your nose
(B7(#11))
GbMAJ7 EbM7 FM7 Bb7
touch - es my fool - ish heart.
C
EbMAJ7 CM7 FM7 Bb7
Love - ly, nev - er ev - er change,
(Db13)
EbMAJ7 C7 FM7 Bb7
keep that breath - less charm. Won't you please ar - range it 'cause I
(A7(#11))
BbM11 Eb7 AbMAJ7 FM7 Bb7
love you, just the way you look to -
Eb6 CM7 FM9 Bb7 Eb6 CM7 FM9 Bb7
night.
(CM7 FM9 Bb7)
FM7 Bb7 Eb6
Just the way you look to - night.
RIT.

WHILE WE'RE YOUNG

WORDS BY BILL ENGVICK
MUSIC BY MORTY PALITZ AND ALEC WILDER

F9 Bb13 Eb6
day, share our
Fm7 Gm7 Cm7 Dm7(b5)
love we must, while we may.
D
G7(b9) Cm7 Bbm7
So blue the skies,
Eb7 Abmaj7 Db9
all sweet sur - prise
Eb6/Bb Ebdim7/Bb Bb9sus Bb7 Eb6
shines be - fore our eyes while we're young.
1 Fm7 Bb7
2

WILLOW WEEP FOR ME

Words and Music by ANN RONELL

FREELY
VERSE:
A+ D9 G9 C13
Oh Lord, why did you send the dark - ness to me?
Oh Lord, is that sweet spell of rap - ture di - vine
F7 Bb13 Eb9 C7(#5)
Are the shad - ows for - ev - er to be? Where's the light I'm long - ing to
that I thought would for - ev - er be mine nev - er more up - on me to
F6 C7 B7(#5) E9 A7
see? Oh love, once we met by the old wil - low
shine? Oh love, here I wait by the wil - low a -
D13 G7 C13
tree, now you've gone and left noth - ing to me,
gain with a heart that knows noth - ing but pain,
F9 D7(#5) G6 Am7 D7 D+
noth - ing but a sweet mem - o - ry. Oh,
but I know I'm wait - ing in vain!
A MED. BALLAD
CHORUS:
G C9 G C9 G Am7 D7
will - ow weep for me, wil - low weep for me, bend your branch - es green a - long the stream
Gone my lov - er's dream, love - ly sum - mer dream, gone and left me here to weep my tears
G Am7 Bbdim7 G/B C9 Am7(b5) D7(#5)
that runs to sea. Lis - ten to my plea, lis - ten wil - low and weep for me.
in - to the stream; sad as I can be, hear me wil - low and weep for me.
G7-13

1
(OPTIONAL D.C.)
2
G C7 G D7(♯5) G DM11 G13
8
CM CM6 GM G13 CM B♭7
Whis-per to the wind and say that love has sinned to leave my heart a-break-ing and
A♭7 G7 CM CM6 GM G13
mak-ing a moan. Mur-mur to the night to hide her star-ry light, so
CM B♭7 A♭7 AM11 D7(♯5)
none will find me sigh-ing and cry-ing all a-lone. Oh,
C
G C9 G C9 G AM7 D7
weep-ing wil-low tree, weep in sym-pa-thy, bend your branch-es down a-long the ground
G AM7 B♭DIM7 G/B C9
and cov-er me. When the sha-dows fall,
AM7(♭5) D7(♯5) G C7 G
bend, oh, wil-low and weep for me.

WITCH HUNT

BY WAYNE SHORTER

FAST SWING
INTRO:
N.C.
E♭MAJ7
FMAJ7
N.C.
GMAJ7
DMAJ7
N.C.
AMAJ7
BMAJ7
G♭MAJ7
A♭MAJ7
D♭MAJ7
MEDIUM SWING
CM7
A
CM11
E♭7
CM11

Gb7
F7
Emaj13
Ebmaj13
Abm11
Amaj7/Ab
To Coda
Abm11
Amaj7/Ab
G7(#9)
8
Solos:
Cm11
Eb7
Cm11
Gb7
F7
Emaj13
Ebmaj13
After last solo D.S. al Coda
Abm11
Amaj7/Ab
Abm11
Amaj7/Ab
G7(#9)
Coda
Abm7

YARDBIRD SUITE

FAST BE-BOP

BY CHARLIE PARKER

A
C6/9 Bb7 C6/9 Bb7 A7
D7 G7 EM7 A7 DM7 G7
C6/9 Bb7 C6/9 Bb7 A7
D7 GSUS C6/9 F#M7(b5) B7(b9)
3
B
EM7 F#M7(b5) B7(b9) EM7 A7
DM7 EM7(b5) A7 D7 DM7 G7
C
C6/9 Bb7 C6/9 Bb7 A7
(A7 DM7 G7)
D7 DM7 G13 C6/9
3

YESTERDAYS

MUSIC BY JEROME KERN
WORDS BY OTTO HARBACH

YOU MUST BELIEVE IN SPRING

MUSIC BY MICHEL LEGRAND
LYRICS BY ALAN AND MARILYN BERGMAN

BALLAD
A
C#m7(b5) F#7(b9) F#7(b9)/B Bm7
When lone - ly feel - ings chill the mea - dows of your mind,
Em7 A7 A7(b9)/D Dmaj7
just think when win - ter comes, can spring be far be - hind?
G#m7(b5) C#7(b9) F#m7(b5) B7(b9)
Be - neath the deep - est snows, the se - cret of a rose
Em7 A7 Dmaj7 G#7(b5) F#7
is mere - ly that it knows you must be - lieve in spring!
B
C#m7(b5) F#7(b9) F#7(b9)/B Bm7
Just as a tree is sure its leaves will re - ap - pear,
Em7 A7 A7(b9)/D Dmaj7
it knows its emp - ti - ness is just a time of year.

G#M7(b5) C#7(b9) GM7(b5) C7(b9)
The fro - zen moun - tain dreams of Ap - ril's melt - ing streams.
(A7(#5))
FM7 Bb7 EbMAJ7 DM7(b5) G7
How cry - stal clear it seems, you must be - lieve in spring!
C
DM7(b5) G7(b9) G7(b9)/C CM7
You must be - lieve in love and trust it's on its way,
FM7 Bb7 Bb7(b9)/Eb EbMAJ7 AM7(b5) D7(b9)
just as the sleep-ing rose a - waits the kiss of May. So in a world of snow,
GM7(b5) C7(b9) FM7 Bb7
of things that come and go, where what you think you know, you
EbMAJ7 AbMAJ9(#11) DM7(b5) G7(b9) CM6
can't be cer - tain of, you must be - lieve in spring and love.
F-9

YOU'D BE SO NICE TO COME HOME TO

FREELY
VERSE:
WORDS AND MUSIC BY COLE PORTER
G7 C6 G/B C9 F Fm
It's not that you're fair - er than a lot of girls just as pleas - in', that I
C G7/D C/E D7 G D7/A G/B D7/A G Eb6
doff my hat as a wor - ship - per at your shrine.___ It's
Bb7 Eb6 Bb/D Eb9 Ab
not that you're rar - er than as - pa - ra - gus out of sea - son, no, my
B Eb/Bb Am7(b5) Ebdim7/Bb Eb/Bb Bdim7 Cm D7 G A E7(b9)
dar - ling, this is the rea - son why you've got to be___ mine: You'd be
A
MEDIUM SWING OR BALLAD
CHORUS:
Am6 Bm7(b5) E7(b9) Am6 Gm9
so nice___ to come home to,___ you'd be so
C7 Fmaj7 Bm7(b5) E7
nice___ by the fire,___ while the breeze on high___ sang a

(Am6)
E7(b9) Am6 F#m7(b5) B7(b9/b5)
lul - la - by, you'd be all that I could de -
8
(F#m7(b5))
Bm7(b5) E7(b9) Am6 Bm7(b5) E7(b9)
sire. Un - der stars, chilled by the
(E7(b9) Am6)
Am6 Gm9 C7
win - ter, un - der an Au - gust moon, burn - ing a -
(Fmaj7 F#dim7 C6/G
Fmaj7 A/E Dm D#dim7 C/E
bove. You'd be so nice, you'd be
Bm7(b5) E7 Am6 D7)
G#dim7 D7/A C/G Ab7 G7 G7(b9)
pa - ra - dise to come home to and
1 2
C6 Bm7(b5) E7(b9) C6/9
love. You'd be love.

YOU STEPPED OUT OF A DREAM

FREELY
VERSE:

MUSIC BY NACIO HERB BROWN
LYRIC BY GUS KAHN

YOU'RE GETTING TO BE A HABIT WITH ME

WORDS BY AL DUBIN
MUSIC BY HARRY WARREN

YOUNG AND FOOLISH

MEDIUM BALLAD

WORDS BY ARNOLD B. HORWITT
MUSIC BY ALBERT HAGUE

COMMON GUITAR CHORDS
Common guitar chords

GUITAR CHORDS

Standard Jazz Chord Voicings *(The root is circled.)*

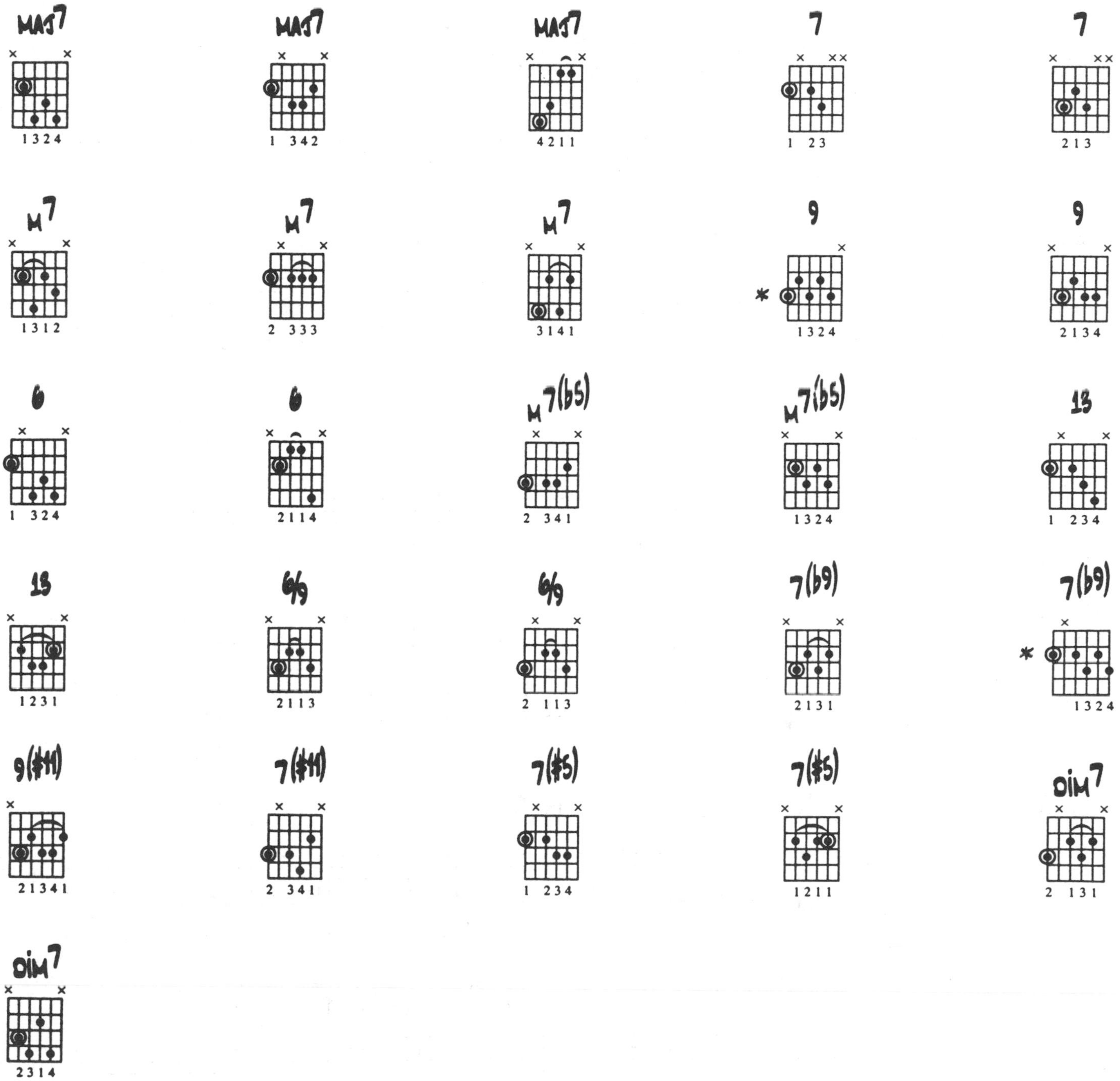
MAJ7
1324
MAJ7
1 342
MAJ7
4211
7
1 23
7
213
M7
1312
M7
2 333
M7
3141
9
*
1324
9
2134
6
1 324
6
2114
M7(b5)
2 341
M7(b5)
1324
13
1 234
13
1231
6/9
2113
6/9
2 113
7(b9)
2131
7(b9)
*
1324
9(#11)
21341
7(#11)
2 341
7(#5)
1 234
7(#5)
1211
DIM7
2 131
DIM7
2314

* Do not play the root.

DISCOGRAPHY
Discography

Following are some suggested recordings of the songs contained in this book.

500 MILES HIGH
Chick Corea/Light as a Feather (Polydor), Stan Getz/Captain Marvel (CBS)
A FELICIDADE
Antonio Carlos Jobim/Composer (Warner Bros.), Black Orpheus/Original Soundtrack (Universal)
AIN'T MISBEHAVIN'
Louis Armstrong (Okeh), Fats Waller (Victor), Nat King Cole (Capitol), Stephane Grappelli (Vanguard)
AIR CONDITIONING
Charlie Parker/Jazz Masters (VRV)
AIREGIN
Rollins, Sonny/The Complete Prestige Recordings (PRS), Miles Davis/Bags' Groove (Prestige), Stan Getz/The Stockholm Concerts (VRV)
AJA
Steely Dan/Aja (MCA)
ALICE IN WONDERLAND
Bill Evans/Sunday at the Village Vanguard (Fantasy), Dave Brubeck/Dave Digs Disney
ALL MY TOMORROWS
Grover Washington Jr./All My Tomorrows (TNK), Nancy Wilson/Yesterday's Love Songs, Today's Blues (BLN)
ALL THE THINGS YOU ARE
Thelonious Monk/Live at the It Club—Complete, Paul Desmond/Gerry Mulligan
ALONE TOGETHER
Bill Evans/The Complete (VRV), Miles Davis/Blue Moods (OJC), Joe Pass/Duets (PAB)
ANA MARIA
Wayne Shorter/Native Dancer (Sony)
ANTHROPOLOGY
Charlie Parker/The Complete Live Performances on Savoy (SVJ), Dizzy Gillespie and the Double Six of Paris (VRV), Ken Burns/Jazz (VRV)
ARMAGEDDON
Wayne Shorter/Night Dreamer (BLN)
AS TIME GOES BY
Dooley Wilson/Cigar Classics: Vol. 1—The Standards (HIPO), Stephane Grappelli/Live at Carnegie Hall (SGN)
AU PRIVAVE
Charlie Parker/Bird: The Complete on Verve, Charlie Parker/Confirmation (VRV), Wynton Marsales/Live at Blues Alley (TNK)
AUTUMN IN NEW YORK
Ella Fitzgerald/The Best Is Yet to Come (OJC), The Capitol Years (Capitol)
AZURE
Duke Ellington/70th Birthday Concert (BLN), Buddy Rich/Big Band Masters (LLT), Tony Bennett Sings Ellington Hot & Cool (TNK), Ella Fitzgerald/The Duke Ellington Songbook (VRV)
BE BOP
Dizzy Gillespie/Something Old, Something New (VRV), John Coltrane/Bags and Trane (Rhino), Charlie Parker/Legendary Dial Masters (Dial)
BERNIE'S TUNE
Mel Torme/In Hollywood (Decca), Charlie Byrd/It's a Wonderful World (CCJ)
BETWEEN THE DEVIL AND THE DEEP BLUE SEA
Benny Goodman/The King of Swing (MSM), Louis Armstrong/Portrait of the Artist as a Young Man (Legacy), Tony Bennett/Who Can I Turn To (TNK)
BEYOND THE SEA
Bobby Darin/As Long as I'm Singing (Rhino), George Benson/20/20 (WBR)
BIRD FEATHERS
Charlie Parker/The Best of Bird (LLT), Legendary Dial Masters (Dial)
BIRD'S NEST
Charlie Parker/Bride of Paradise (ECL), Legendary Dial Masters (Dial)
BLACK NILE
Wayne Shorter/Jazz Profile No. 20 (BLN), Night Dreamer (BLN)
BLACKBERRY WINTER
Keith Jarrett/Mysteries (GRP)
BLUE AND SENTIMENTAL
Count Basie/Swingstation (GRP), Best of (CAP), Buddy Rich/This One's for Basie (VRV)
BLUE 'N' BOOGIE
Charlie Parker/Yardbird Suite: The Ultimate Charlie Parker (Rhino)
BLUE RONDO A LA TURK
Dave Brubeck/Time Out, Blue Rondo (CCJ), Al Jarreau/Breakin' Away (WBR)
BLUE TRAIN
John Coltrane/The Art of John Coltrane (BLN), Blue Train (BLN), Dave Grusin/GRP All-Star Big Band Live! (GRP)
BLUES FOR ALICE
Charlie Parker/Swedish Schnapps (VRV), Confirmation (VRV)
BLUESETTE
Toots Thielemans/Verve Jazz Masters (VRV), Mel Torme/'Round Midnight (Stash)
BODY AND SOUL
Carly Simon/Torch (WBR), Billy Eckstine (MGM), Bill Evans (WB), Billie Holiday (Columbia, Verve)
BONGO BEEP
Charlie Parker/The Legendary Dial Masters (JazzClassics)
BONGO BOP
Charlie Parker/The Legendary Dial Masters (JazzClassics)
THE BOULEVARD OF BROKEN DREAMS
Tony Bennett/All-Time Greatest Hits (TNK), Diana Krall/All for You (GRP)
BUT BEAUTIFUL
Bill Evans/Since We Met (Fantasy), Billie Holiday/Lady in Satin (Sony)
BYE, BYE, BLACKBIRD
John Coltrane/Best Of (PAB), Ricki Lee Jones/Pop Pop (GFN), Tony Bennett/Forty Years, The Artistry of (LGY)
CANTALOUPE ISLAND
Herbie Hancock/Cantaloupe Island (BLN), Empyrean Isles (BLN)
CARAVAN
Tony Bennett/Sings Ellington Hot & Cool (TNK), Duke Ellington/Ken Burns Jazz (Sony)
CAST YOUR FATE TO THE WIND (Instrumental Version)
Vince Guaraldi/Greatest Hits (FSY), The Best o David Benoit (GRP)
CENTRAL PARK WEST
John Coltrane/Coltrane's Sound (Atlantic), Jim Bruno/Burnin' (Concord Jazz)
CHAMELEON
Herbie Hancock/Greatest Hits (TNK)
CHEGA DE SAUDADE
Jobim/Most Beautiful Songs (IRR), João Gilberto/Chega De Saudade (EMI)
A CHILD IS BORN
Thad Jones/Mel Lewis/Sonny Lester Collection (LRC), Ultimate Joe Williams (VRV), Roland Hanna/Perugia (FRD)
CHRISTMAS TIME IS HERE
Vince Guaraldi/Greatest Hits (FSY)
COME BACK TO ME
Cherry Poppin' Daddies/Zoot Suit Riot (RSL), Sammy Davis Jr./Yes I Can (WAR)
COME SUNDAY
Duke Ellington/The Best of the Duke Ellington Centennial Edition (RCV), Joe Pass/Virtuoso (PAB), Bucky Pizzarelli/April Kisses (ABO)
CONFIRMATION
Charlie Parker/Yardbird Suite: The Ultimate Charlie Parker Collection (Rhino), Charlie Parker/Ken Burns Jazz (VRV), Art Pepper/Birds and Monks (GXY)
COOL BLUES
Charlie Parker/Very Best of Bird (WBR), The Legendary Dial Masters (Dial)
COTTONTAIL
Duke Ellington/The Ellington Legacy, Count Basie Orchestra/Count Plays Duke (MAF), Duk Ellington/Ken Burns Jazz (Sony)
COUNTDOWN
John Coltrane/Legendary Jazz (Atlantic), Giant Steps (ATL)
CRYSTAL SILENCE
Chick Corea/Crystal Silence (ECM), Return to Forever (ECM)
CUTE
Count Basie/Best of the Roulette Years, Jimmy McGriff/Tribute to Basie (LLT)
A DAY IN THE LIFE OF A FOOL
Vince Guaraldi/Greatest Hits (Fantasy), Frank Sinatra/My Way (Reprise)
THE DAYS OF WINE AND ROSES
Henry Mancini (RCA), Tony Bennett/Bill Evans (Fantasy), Frank Sinatra (Reprise)
DEACON BLUES
Steely Dan/Aja (MCA)
DESAFINADO
Jobim/The Man From Ipanema (VRV), Art Pepper/The Complete Galaxy Recordings (GXY
DEXTERITY
Charlie Parker/Very Best of Bird (WBR), The Legendary Dial Masters (Dial)
DIZZY ATMOSPHERE
Dizzy Gillespie/Dizzy Atmosphere (DRV), Char Parker/Yardbird Suite: The Ultimate Charlie Parker Collection (Rhino)
DO IT AGAIN
Steely Dan/Can't Buy a Thrill (MCA)

O NOTHIN' TILL YOU HEAR FROM ME
ony Bennett Sings Ellington (Columbia)
OLPHIN DANCE
erbie Hancock/Maiden Voyage (BLN), Jaco astorius/Live in NYC, Vol. 4 (Big World)
ON'T BLAME ME
at King Cole/The Complete Early Transcriptions Vintage), Etta James/These Foolish Things MCA), Charlie Parker/Best of Bird (WBR)
ON'T EXPLAIN
illie Holiday/Back to Back (Ember), John oltrane/The Prestige Recordings (PRS)
ON'T GET AROUND MUCH ANYMORE
ony Bennett Sings Ellington (Columbia)
ONNA LEE
harlie Parker/Yardbird Suite: The Ultimate harlie Parker Collection (Rhino), Joe Pass/Guitar irtuoso (PAB)
RIFTING ON A REED
harlie Parker/The Legendary Dial Masters (Jazz lassics)
HE DUKE
ave Brubeck/Plays Brubeck (LGY), Dave rubeck/Ken Burns Jazz (Sony), Joe Pass/My ong (TLR)
UKE'S PLACE (C Jam Blues)
uke Ellington/Priceless Jazz Collection (GRP), harlie Mingus/At Carnegie Hall (Rhino), Duke llington and Count Basie/Battle of the ands (LGY)
ARLY AUTUMN
el Torme/At the Red Hill/Live at the aisonette, Ella Fitzgerald/Sings the Johnny ercer Songbook (VRV)
ASY TO LOVE
harlie Parker (VRV), Billie Holiday (VRV), rank Sinatra (Reprise)
MBRACEABLE YOU
rank Sinatra/Duets/Duets II (Capitol), Nat King ole (Capitol), Charlie Parker (Prestige)
MILY
ony Bennett/Forty Years: The Artistry Of Legacy)
PISTROPHY
helonious Monk/This Is Jazz #5 (LGY), Miles avis/Jazz Greatest Hits (TNK)
SP
iles Davis/ESP, Charles Mingus and Friends in oncert (TNK)
UROPA
antana/Best of Santana (LGY), Gato arbieri/Greatest Hits (A&M)
VERYTIME WE SAY GOODBYE
inah Washington/The Masters (Eagleroc), Ray harles & Betty Carter/Dedicated to You (Rhino)
ALL
iles Davis/Nefertiti (LGY)
ALLING IN LOVE WITH LOVE
oe Williams/Now & Then (SBZ), Tony Bennett/If Ruled the World: Song for the Jet Set (TNK)
ASCINATIN' RHYTHM
lla Fitzgerald/Gershwin Songbook (Verve), osemary Clooney/Sings the Lyrics of Ira ershwin (CCJ)
FINE ROMANCE
lla Fitzgerald/The Jerome Kern Songbook Verve)
FOGGY DAY
rank Sinatra/The Complete Reprise Studio ecordings (RPS)

FOOTPRINTS
Shorter/Adam's Apple (BLN), Miles Davis/Miles Smiles (LGY)
FOUR
Miles Davis/Miles Davis and the Jazz Giants (PRS), Mel Torme/Round Midnight: A Retrospective (Stash)
FREEDOM JAZZ DANCE
Eddie Harris/Greater Than the Sum of His Parts (32 Jazz), Miles Davis/Miles Smiles (LGY)
GEE BABY, AIN'T I BEEN GOOD TO YOU
Nat King Cole/The Best of (Capitol), Ella Fitzgerald/Compact Jazz (Verve), Diana Krall/All for You (GRP)
THE GENTLE RAIN
Bonfa/Non-Stop to Brazil (CKY), George Benson/Beyond the Blue Horizon (LGY)
GIANT STEPS
John Coltrane/Legendary Jazz (Rhino), John Patitucci/Now (CCJ), Arturo Sandoval/Dream Come True (GRP)
THE GIRL FROM IPANEMA
Astrud Gilberto/The Girl From Ipanema (VRV), Getz/Gilberto (VRV)
GIRL TALK
Tony Bennett/The Movie Song Album (Sony), George Shearing/Once Again (TelArc), Mel Torme and Cleo Lane/Nothing Without You (Concord Jazz)
GOOD BAIT
John Coltrane/Soultrane (PRS), Dizzie Gillespie/Something Old, Something New (VRV)
GOOD MORNING, HEARTACHE
Billie Holiday/Ultimate Billie Holiday (VRV), Ella Fitzgerald/Four by Four (VRV)
GROOVIN' HIGH
Dizy Gillespie/Shaw 'Nuff (MCA), Charlie Parker/Newly Discovered Sides By (SVJ)
HAVE YOU MET MISS JONES
Louis Armstrong/I've Got the World on a String/Louis Under the Stars (VRV)
HERE'S THAT RAINY DAY
Oscar Peterson/At the Montreux Jazz Festival (OJC), Dave Brubeck/Triple Play (TLR)
HIT THAT JIVE JACK
Diana Krall/All for You (GRP), Nat King Cole/ Hit That Jive Jack (Decca/Jazz)
HONEYSUCKLE ROSE
Fats Waller/Ain't Misbehavin' (LLT), Anita O'Day/Compact Jazz (VRV)
HOT HOUSE
Charlie Parker/The Complete Live Performances On Savoy (SVJ), Dizzy Gillespie/Shaw Nuff (MCF)
HOW HIGH THE MOON
Les Paul & Mary Ford/Sentimental Journey: Pop Vocal Classics (Rhino)
HOW INSENSITIVE
Frank Sinatra/Francis Albert Sinatra & Antonio Carlos Jobim (Reprise)
HOW LONG HAS THIS BEEN GOING ON
Charlie Byrd/Mr. Guitar (OJC), Ella Fitzgerald/Sings the Gershwin Song Book (VRV)
I CAN'T GET STARTED
Billie Holiday/The Legacy 1933–58 (Legacy), Frank Sinatra/Concepts (Capitol)
I COULD WRITE A BOOK
Ella Fitzgerald/Rodgers and Hart Songbook V. 2 (VRV)

I DON'T STAND A GHOST OF A CHANCE WITH YOU
Diana Krall/Love Scenes
I GOT IT BAD (And That Ain't Good)
Duke Ellington/The Popular Duke Ellington (RCA/Victor), John Coltrane/The Prestige Recordings (PRS)
I GOT RHYTHM
Lena Horne/Love Is the Thing (RCA)
I GOTTA RIGHT TO SING THE BLUES
Billie Holiday/Compact Jazz (VRV), Wynton Marsalis/Standard Time Vol. 2 (TNK), Frank Sinatra/Concepts (CAP)
I HEAR A RHAPSODY
Bill Evans/Live at Montreux II (Sony), Anita O'Day/Swing Time in Hawaii (M&H)
I LET A SONG GO OUT OF MY HEART
Tony Bennett/Jazz (TNK), Kenny Burrell/Ellington Is Forever (Fantasy), Erroll Garner/Jazz 'Round Midnight (Verve)
I LOVE PARIS
Ella Fitzgerald/Cole Porter Songbook (VRV), Charlie Parker/Bird: The Complete on Verve (VRV), Frank Sinatra/Sings Cole Porter (Goldrush)
I LOVE YOU
Chet Baker/With Strings (LGY), Bill Evans/Complete Fantasy Recordings (FSY)
I MISS YOU
Diana Krall/Love Scenes
I SHOULD CARE
Paul Desmond/Complete RCA Recordings (RCA), Bill Evans/Trio at Town Hall (VRV)
I'LL BE AROUND
Tony Bennett/Forty Years: The Artistry Of (LGY), Mel Torme/My Night to Dream (CCJ)
I'LL REMEMBER APRIL
Chet Baker (Verve), Wynton Marsalis/Standard Time V. 2 (TNK), Charlie Parker/With Strings (Verve), Frank Sinatra/The Complete Capitol Single Collection (Capitol)
I'M AN ERRAND GIRL FOR RHYTHM
Diana Krall/All for You (GRPI)
I'M BEGINNING TO SEE THE LIGHT
Kenny Burrell/Ellington Is Forever (FSY), Ella Fitzgerald/Duke Ellington Songbook (VRV)
IMPRESSIONS
John Coltrane/Traces of Trane (JMY), Impressions (Impulse), McCoy Tyner/Trident (FSY)
IN A MELLOW TONE
Duke Ellington/Ellington: This Is Jazz #7 (LGY), Joe Pass/Portraits of Duke Ellington (PAB)
IN A SENTIMENTAL MOOD
Duke Ellington/Ellington: This Is Jazz #7 (LGY), Grover Washington Jr./Then and Now (TNK), Tony Bennett Sings Duke Ellington (Columbia)
IN WALKED BUD
Monk/Best of the Blue Note Years (BLN), Tito Puente/Out of This World (CJP)
IN YOUR OWN SWEET WAY
Dave Brubeck/Young Lions and Old Tigers (TLR), Bill Evans/The Original Jazz Classic Showcase Series (OJC), Sonny Rollins/The Complete Prestige Recordings (PRS)
INVITATION
Bill Evans/Complete Fantasy Recordings (FSY), Joe Sample/Invitation (WBR), Dinah Washington/Blue Gardenia: Songs of Love (EMR), Jaco Pastorious/Invitation (WB)

IS YOU IS OR IS YOU AIN'T (Ma Baby)
Louis Jordan/Greatest Hits (MSP), Nat King Cole/Tri Recordings (LLT), Diana Krall/Only Trust Your Heart (GRP)
THE ISLAND
David Benoit/Letter to Evan (GRP)
IT DON'T MEAN A THING (If It Ain't Got That Swing)
Duke Ellington/Greatest Hits (RCA/Vict), Tony Bennett/MTV Unplugged (TNK)
IT'S A RAGGY WALTZ
Dave Brubeck/Greatest Hits (LGY)
IT'S ONLY A PAPER MOON
Basie & Zoot (OJC), John Pizzarelli/Dear Mr. Cole (NVS), Frank Sinatra/Swing and Dance (TNK)
I'VE GOT YOU UNDER MY SKIN
Frank Sinatra/The Complete Reprise Studio Recordings (Reprise)
JAVA JIVE
The Ink Spots/The Anthology (MCA)
JOSIE
Steely Dan/Aja (MCA)
JUST FRIENDS
Charlie Parker/Yardbird Suite: The Ultimate Charlie Parker Collection (Rhino), Tony Bennett: Tony Sings for Two (CBSColle)
KID CHARLEMAGNE
Steely Dan/The Royal Scam (MCA)
LA FIESTA
Chick Corea/Return to Forever (ECM), Stan Getz/Captain Marvel (CBS)
LADY SINGS THE BLUES
Billie Holiday/Ultimate Jazz (VRV), Ella Fitzgerald/Ultimate Divas (VRV)
THE LAMP IS LOW (Pavane)
Harry James/The Complete Recordings (TNK), Sarah Vaughan/Jazz Fest Masters (Volcano)
LAURA
Frank Sinatra/Sings His Greatest Hits (Legacy), Charlie Parker/Big Band (Verve), Dave Brubeck/Greatest Hits From the Fantasy Years (Fantasy)
LAZYBIRD
John Coltrane/Blue Train (Blue Note)
LESTER LEAPS IN
Lester Young/This Is Jazz #26 (TNK), Charlie Parker/Talkin' Bird (VRV)
LI'L DARLIN'
Count Basie/Atomic Swing (BLN), Kenny Burrell (Concord Jazz), George Benson (Atlantic), Oscar Peterson (Verve)
LIMEHOUSE BLUES
Cannonball Adderley/Ultimate (Verve)
Duke Ellington/1931–1932 (CCS), Benny Goodman/On the Air 37–38 (Legacy)
Lionel Hampton/The Legendary Decca Recordings (GRP)
LINUS AND LUCY
Vince Guaraldi/Greatest Hits (FSY), Wynton Marsalis/Joe Cool's Blues (TNK), David Benoit/Smooth Sounds (RZT)
LITTLE AFRICAN FLOWER
Bill Mays/An Ellington Affair (Concord Jazz)
LITTLE BOAT (O Barquinho)
Gabor Zabo/The Sorcerer (GRP), Charlie Byrd/Brazilian Byrd, Leila Pinheiro/Benção/Bossa Nova (Phillipps)
LOVE IS HERE TO STAY
Nat King Cole (Capitol), Harry Connick, Jr. (Columbia), Ella Fitzgerald & Louis Armstrong (Verve)
LOVER MAN
Billie Holiday/Back to Back (Ember)
LULLABY OF BIRDLAND
George Shearing/Once Again That Shearing Sound (TLR), Mel Torme/A Very Special Time (AVE), Duke Ellington/The Jeep Is Jumpin' (Magnumco)
LUSH LIFE
Chet Baker/Romance (BLN), Nat King Cole/Lush Life (CAP), Ella Fitzgerald/Duke Ellington Songbook (VRV)
MAIDEN VOYAGE
Herbie Hancock/This Is Jazz #35 (LGY), Maynard Ferguson/Verve Jazz Masters (VRV)
MAKIN' WHOOPIE
Ella Fitzgerald/First Lady of Song (VRV)
THE MAN I LOVE
Peggy Lee/Spotlight (Capitol), Billie Holiday (Columbia), Charlie Parker (Verve)
MEDITATION
Antonio Carlos Jobim/Jazz 'Round Midnight (Verve), Charlie Byrd/The Bossa Nova Years (CJP), Astrud Gilberto/The Silver Collection (Verve)
MINNIE THE MOOCHER
Cab Calloway/Bands of the '30s (Intersound)
MISS OTIS REGRETS
Ella Fitzgerald/The Cole Porter Songbook (VRV), Ellis Marsalis, Loved Ones (TNK)
MISTER FIVE BY FIVE
Harry James/Bandstand Memories 38–48 (HNS), Andrews Sisters
MISTY
Johnny Mathis/The Ultimate Hits Collection (Legacy)
MOMENT'S NOTICE
John Coltrane/The Ultimate Blue Trane (BLN), Harry Connick, Jr./25 (TNK)
MOOD INDIGO
Tony Bennett/Sings Ellington Hot & Cool (TNK), Duke Ellington/This Is Jazz #7 (LGY)
MOONLIGHT IN VERMONT
Tony Bennett/Here's to the Ladies (TNK), Mel Torme/In Hollywood (Decca), Billie Holiday/All or Nothing at All (Verve)
THE MORE I SEE YOU
Nat King Cole/If I Give My Heart to You (EMI), Chet Baker (Riverside), Dick Haymes/Best Of (Curb), Chris Montez/Bachelor Pad Pleasures (CHRO)
MR. LUCKY
Sarah Vaughan/The Mancini Songbook (VRV)
MR. PC
John Coltrane/Legendary Jazz (Atlantic)
MY FOOLISH HEART
Bill Evans/At the Village Vanguard (RVS)
MY FUNNY VALENTINE
Miles Davis/Greatest Hits (LGY), Bill Evans/Undercurrent (BLN)
MY ROMANCE
Bucky and John Pizzarelli/Contrasts (ABO), The Complete Ella Fitzgerald Song Books (VRV), Bill Evans/At the Village Vanguard (FSY), Waltz for Debbie (FSY)
MY SHIP
Miles Davis/Love Songs (LGY), Sonny Rollins/The Standard Sonny Rollins (RCV)
MYSTERIOUS TRAVELER
Weather Report/This Is Jazz #10 (LGY)
NAIMA
John Coltrane/The Very Best of John Coltrane, Carlos Santana/Dance of the Rainbow Serpent (LGY)
NATURE BOY
Nat King Cole, Legends of the 20th Century (CAP), Miles Davis/Blue Moods (OJC)
NEFERTITI
Herbie Hancock/A Jazz Collection (LGY), Miles Davis/Nefertiti (LGY)
NIGHT AND DAY
Dionne Warrick/Sings Cole Porter (ARI), Frank Sinatra/Greatest Hits (RCA)
A NIGHT IN TUNISIA
Charlie Parker/Legendary Dial Masters (Dial), Masters of Jazz V. 6 (1947), Young Bird, Dizzy Gillespie/Masters of Jazz V. 7 (1946)
NIGHT TRAIN
Ricki Lee Jones (WBR), Wynton Marsalis/Big Train (TNK), Jimmy Smith and Wes Montgomery/Dynamic Duo ((VRV)
OH, LADY BE GOOD
John Pizzarelli/One Night With You (Chesky), Django Reinhardt/Swing Jazz (Music Club)
OLD DEVIL MOON
Tony Bennett/MTV Unplugged (TNK), Miles Davis/The Complete Prestige Recordings (PRS)
OLEO
Sonny Rollins/The Complete Prestige Recording (PRS), Miles Davis/Relaxin' With the Miles Dav Quintet (OJC), Joe Pass/Chops (OJC)
ON A CLEAR DAY (You Can See Forever)
Sarah Vaughan/The Complete Sarah Vaughan on Mercury (Vol. 4), Bill Evans/Alone (VRV)
ON GREEN DOLPHIN STREET
Tony Bennett/Jazz (TNK), Harry Connick, Jr. (TNK), Oscar Peterson/Very Tall (VRV)
ONE NOTE SAMBA
Jobim/Verve Jazz Masters: The Bossa Nova Story (VRV), Stan Getz/Jazz Samba (VRV)
OO-SHOO-BE-DO-BE
Dizzy Gillespie/The Champ (SVJ)
ORNITHOLOGY
Parker/Yardbird Suite: Ultimate Charlie Parker Collection (Rhino), Bill Evans/The Solo Sessions Vol. 2 (MLS)
OUR DELIGHT
Tad Dameron/The Magic Touch (OJC), Fats Navarro/Everything's Cool (PAL)
OVER THE RAINBOW
Absolutely everyone has recorded this song! But check out Judy Garland's version for inspiration.
PEG
Steely Dan/Aja (MCA)
PERDIDO
Duke Ellington/Verve Jazz Masters 4 (VRV), Dinah Washington/The Swingin' Miss "D" (VRV
Count Basie/Kansas City 5 (OJC)
PETER GUNN
Henry Mancini/All-Time Greatest Hits, Vol. 1 (RCA), Dave Grusin/Two for the Road (GRP)
POINCIANNA
Gato Barbieri/Greatest Hits (A&M), Dave Brubeck/Bravo (LGY), Ahmad Jamal/At the Pershing (Chess)

OLKA DOTS AND MOONBEAMS
unt Basie/At Newport (RV), Charlie
rd/Moments Like This (CCJ), Mel Torme/A
ry Special Time (AVE)
RELUDE TO A KISS
ny Bennett/Sings Duke Ellington (Columbia)
UASIMODO
arlie Parker/Bluebird (ECL), The Legendary
al Masters
UIET NIGHTS OF QUIET STARS (orcovado)
an Getz & João Gilberto/Getz, Gilberto (Verve),
ancis Albert Sinatra & Antonio Carlos Jobim
eprise)
UIET NOW
ll Evans/At Half Moon Bay (MLS)
ELAXIN' AT CAMARILLO
harlie Parker/Bird of Paradise (ECL), Joe
ss/Guitar Virtuoso (PAB)
'ROUND MIDNIGHT
helonious Monk/Best of the Blue Note Years
LN), Wes Montgomery/The Artistry of Wes
ontgomery (RVS)
ABIA
bim/Stone Flower (LGY)
ALT PEANUTS
zzy Gillespie/Shaw 'Nuff (MCF), Diz 'n' Bird
Carnegie Hall (BLN)
ATIN DOLL
la Fitzgerald & Duke Ellington/Ella & Basie
erve)
CRAPPLE FROM THE APPLE
harlie Parker/Very Best of Bird (WBR), John
oltrane/Jazz Sax Classics (Rhino)
ECRET LOVE
oris Day/The Essence Of (Legacy), Ahmad
mal (Argo), Joe Pass (Pablo), Johnny Mathis
Columbia)
KYLARK
inda Ronstadt/Lush Life (ELK), Bette Midler
tlantic), Paul Desmond (CBS), Jim Hall
Concord Jazz)
O NICE (Summer Samba)
ergio Mendes/Best Of, Astrud Gilberto/Talkin'
/RV)
OLAR
iles Davis/Jazz Showcase (CUC), Pat
etheny/Question and Answer (GFN)
OLITUDE
uke Ellington/The Popular Duke Ellington
RCV), Tony Bennett/On Holiday (TNK), Billie
oliday/Ultimate Billie Holiday (VRV)
OME OTHER BLUES
ohn Coltrane/Coltrane Jazz (Atlantic)
OME OTHER TIME
ony Bennett/Forty Years: The Artistry of Tony
ennett (LGY), Bill Evans/Everybody Digs Bill
vans (JVC)
OMEONE TO WATCH OVER ME
inda Ronstadt/'Round Midnight/The Nelson
iddle Sessions (ELK), Willie Nelson
Columbia), Charlie Parker (Verve)
HE SONG IS YOU
het Baker/The Pacific Jazz Years (PCJ), Stan
etz/The Song Is You (LLT), Charlie Parker/The
ssential Charlie Parker (VRV)
OPHISTICATED LADY
Duke Ellington/Greatest Hits (RCV), Billie
Holiday/All or Nothing at All (VRV)

SPAIN
Chick Corea/Light as a Feather (Polydor), Al Jarreau/Best Of (WBR)
SPEAK LOW
Billie Holiday/All or Nothing at All (VRV), Diane Schur/The Very Best Of (GRP)
SPRING CAN REALLY HANG YOU UP THE MOST
David Benoit/Letter to Evan (GRP), Ella Fitzgerald/Clap Hands, Here Comes Charlie (VRV)
ST. THOMAS
Sonny Rollins/The Complete RCA Victor Recordings of Sonny Rollins (RCV), Branford Marsalis/Renaissance (TNK)
STAIRWAY TO THE STARS
Chet Baker/The Art of the Ballad (PRS), Oscar Peterson/The Complete Young Oscar Peterson (RCA), Ella Fitzgerald/The Best of Ella Fitzgerald (Decca Jazz)
STAR EYES
Joe Pass/Guitar Virtuoso (PAB), Chet Baker/The Italian Sessions (RCV)
STARDUST
Hoagy Carmichael/Ole Buttermilk Sky (CollChoi), Duke Ellington/The Complete Capital Recordings (Mosaic)
STOMPIN' AT THE SAVOY
Ella Fitzgerald/The Complete Ella Fitzgerald & Louis Armstrong on Verve (VRV), Benny Goodman/All-Time Greatest Hits (TNK), Mel Torme/Spotlight on Mel Torme (CAP)
STRAIGHTEN UP AND FLY RIGHT
Diana Krall/Stepping Out (Justin Time), Natalie Cole/Unforgettable (Elektra)
STREET OF DREAMS
Tony Bennett/Jazz (TNK), Cannonball Adderley/Verve Jazz Masters (VRV)
STRUTTIN' WITH SOME BARBEQUE
Louis Armstrong/The Complete Hot Five (Sony)
SUMMERTIME
Ella Fitzgerald/Pure Ella (Verve), Chet Baker/Chet in Paris (VRV), Paul Desmond/Best Of (CTI), Bill Evans/Complete Riverside Recordings (RVS)
SWEET GEORGIA BROWN
Oscar Peterson/Live at the Bluenote (TLR), Ella Fitzgerald/Compact Jazz (VRV), Django Reinhardt/Verve Jazz Masters (VRV)
SWEET LORRAINE
Chet Baker/Plays (PCJ), Tony Bennett/This Is Jazz #33 (TNK)
TAIN'T NOBODY'S BUSINESS (If I Do)
Billie Holiday/The Complete Decca Recordings (GRP)
TAKE FIVE
Dave Brubeck/Take Five (LGY)
TEACH ME TONIGHT
Al Jarreau/Breakin' Away (Warner Bros.) Nat King Cole/The Billy May Sessions (Capitol), Natalie Cole/Stardust (Elektra), Etta James/Time After Time (PVM)
TENOR MADNESS
Sonny Rollins/Tenor Madness (DCC), John Coltrane/The Prestige Recordings (PRS)
THAT OLD FEELING
Dinah Washington/In Love (ROU), Louis Armstrong/An American Icon (HIPO)
THEY CAN'T TAKE THAT AWAY FROM ME
Ella Fitzgerald & Louis Armstrong/The Complete Gershwin Songbooks (Verve), Frank Sinatra/Duets & Duets II (Capitol)

THIS CAN'T BE LOVE
Diana Krall/Stepping Out (Justin Time)
THIS MASQUERADE
George Benson/The Best of George Benson (WBR), David Sanborn/Pearls (ELK)
TIME AFTER TIME
Tony Bennett/Perfectly Frank (TNK), John Coltrane/Stardust (OJC)
TIMES LIE
Chick Corea & Stan Getz/Captain Marvel (KOJ)
TONES FOR JOAN'S BONES
Chick Corea/Mountains in the Clouds (CTB)
TUNE UP
Miles Davis/Blue Haze (CJC), Sonny Rollins/The Best of Sonny Rollins: The Blue Note Years (BLN)
TWISTED
Annie Ross/Music Is Forever (DRG), Joni Mitchell/Court and Spark (Elektra), Lambert, Ross & Hendricks/Everybody's Boppin' (Sony)
VALSE HOT
Sonny Rollins/The Original Jazz Classic Showcase Series (OJC)
WATCH WHAT HAPPENS
Ella Fitzgerald/Sunshine of Your Love (VRV), Lena Horne/Watch What Happens! (DCC Jazz), Tony Bennett/If I Ruled the World: Song for the Jet Set (TNK)
WATERMELON MAN
Herbie Hancock/Backtracks
THE WAY YOU LOOK TONIGHT
Dave Brubeck and Paul Desmond (Fantasy), Wes Montgomery/Complete Riverside Recordings (Riverside), Mel Torme/A Special Time (AVE)
WHILE WE'RE YOUNG
Bill Evans/The Complete Fantasy Recordings (FSY), Wes Montgomery/While We're Young (Milestone)
WILLOW WEEP FOR ME
Tony Bennett/On Holiday (TNK)
Billie Holiday/The Complete (Verve)
WINDOWS
Chick Corea/The Best of Chick Corea (BLN), Stan Getz/Verve Jazz Masters (VRV)
WITCH HUNT
Shorter, Wayne/Speak No Evil (Blue Note)
YARDBIRD SUITE
Charlie Parker/Bird Symbols (CTB)
YESTERDAYS
Billie Holiday/History of the Real Billie Holiday (VRV), Miles Davis/The Ballad Artistry Of, Ella Fitzgerald/The Complete Ella Fitzgerald Song Books (VRV)
YOU MUST BELIEVE IN SPRING
Tony Bennett/Together Again (DRG), Bill Evans/You Must Believe in Spring (WB)
YOU STEPPED OUT OF A DREAM
Dave Brubeck/24 Classic Original Recordings (Fantasy), Nat King Cole/Lush Life (Capitol), John Pizzarelli/Naturally (NVS)
YOU'D BE SO NICE TO COME HOME TO
Nancy Wilson/Spotlight on Nancy Wilson (CAP), Cannonball Adderley/Verve Jazz Masters (VRV)
YOUNG AND FOOLISH
Bill Evans/Everybody Digs Bill Evans (JVC)
YOU'RE GETTING TO BE A HABIT WITH ME
Diana Krall/Love Scenes

COMMON CHORD VOICINGS
Common chord voicings

Included here are some common piano voicings all based on a C root. Occasionally, we have displayed more than or inversion of the same chord that may be particularly useful. Of course, as with all fakebooks, you should use the vo ing best suited to your needs.

Major

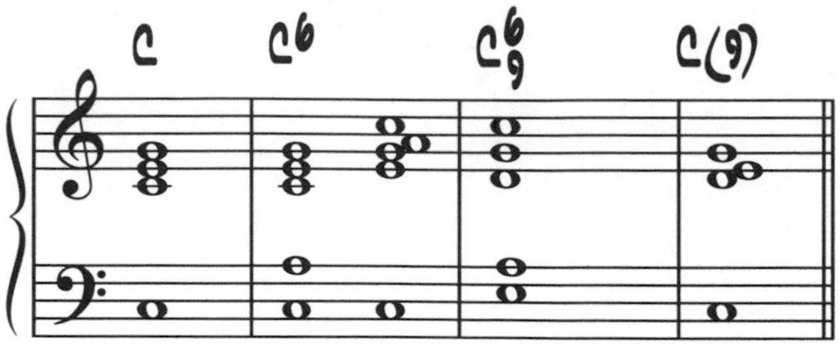

Minor

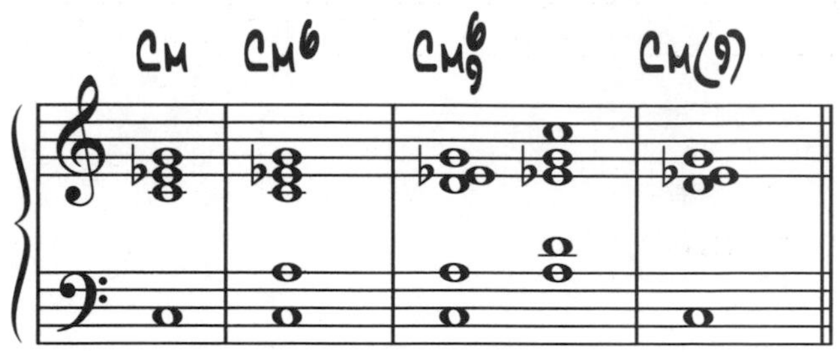

Augmented/Diminished

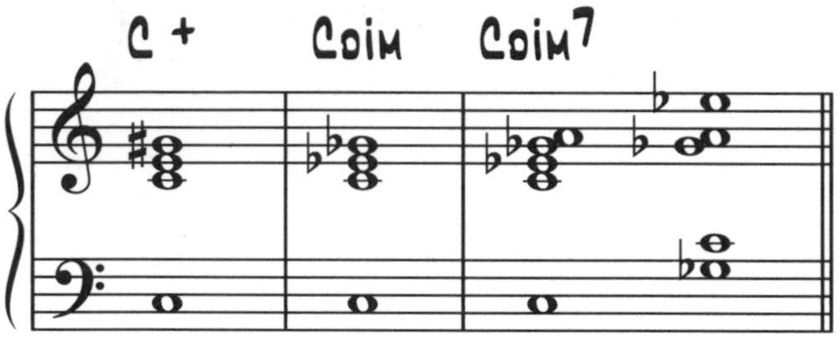

Minor

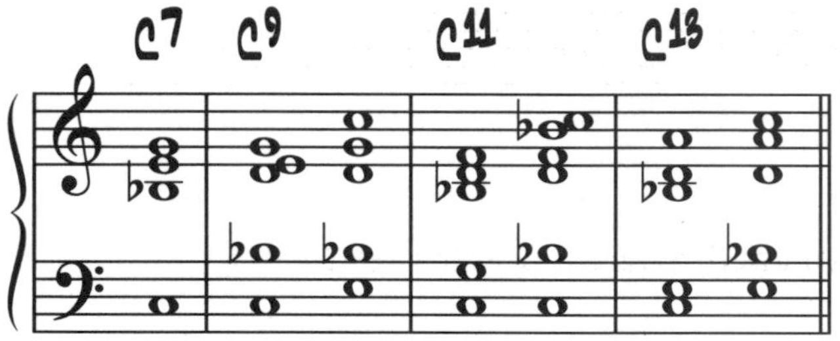

Maj 7th

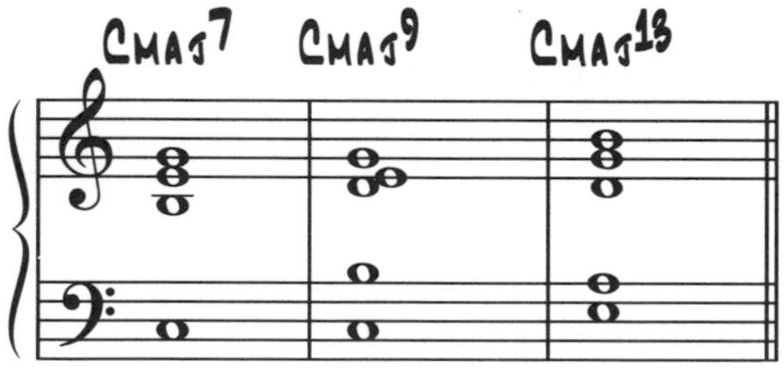

Extended/Altered Maj 7th

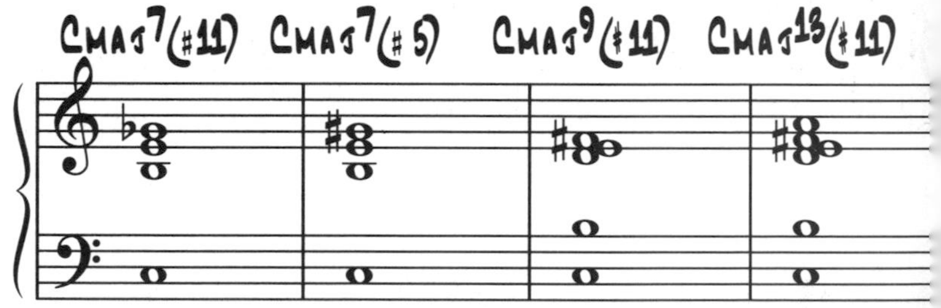

Minor

Extended/Altered Minor 7th

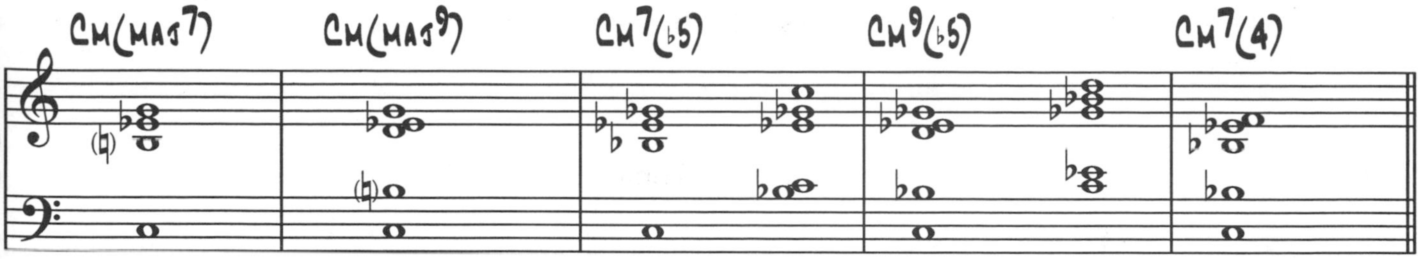

Suspended

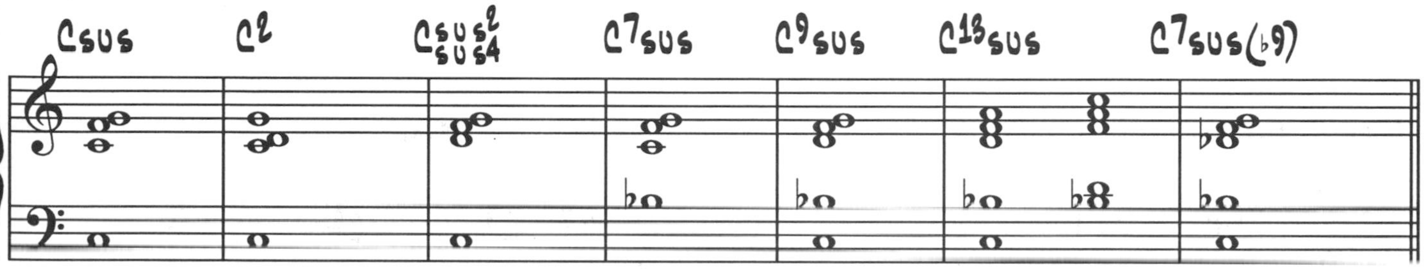

Extended/Altered Dominant 7th

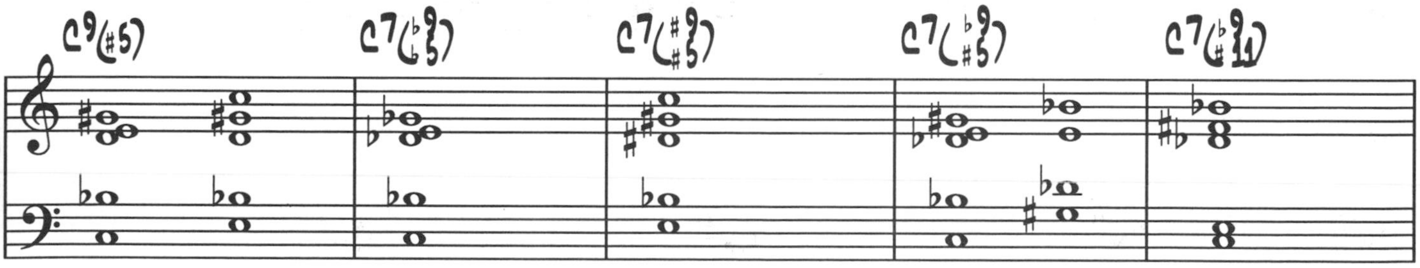

CHORD SUBSTITUTIONS

The chord names used in this fakebook are, for the most part, either the original chords used by the composer or variations that are so common that they supercede the original. Sometimes we have also listed widely used substitutions or reharmonizations based on the original "changes" displayed in parentheses above the main changes. These substitutions can vary greatly in complexity, ranging from a simple adding of chord tones (Ex. 1) to wholesale reharmonization of an entire phrase. The variations you choose to use are entirely personal, and in this way you can often make your arrangement of a song quite unique.

Displayed below are a few examples of some commonly used chord substitutions.

Added Extensions
Adding or extending chord tones changes the harmony.

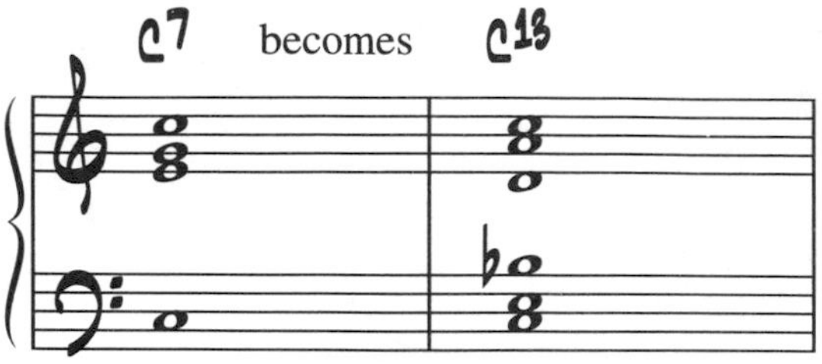

Tritone Substitution
Where a dominant 7th or minor 7th chord is replaced by a dominant 7th chord whose root is a tritone away from the original. A tritone is defined as the interval of the augmented 4th or diminished 5th (three whole tones.) The example shown below uses both the original chords and their tritone substitutions.

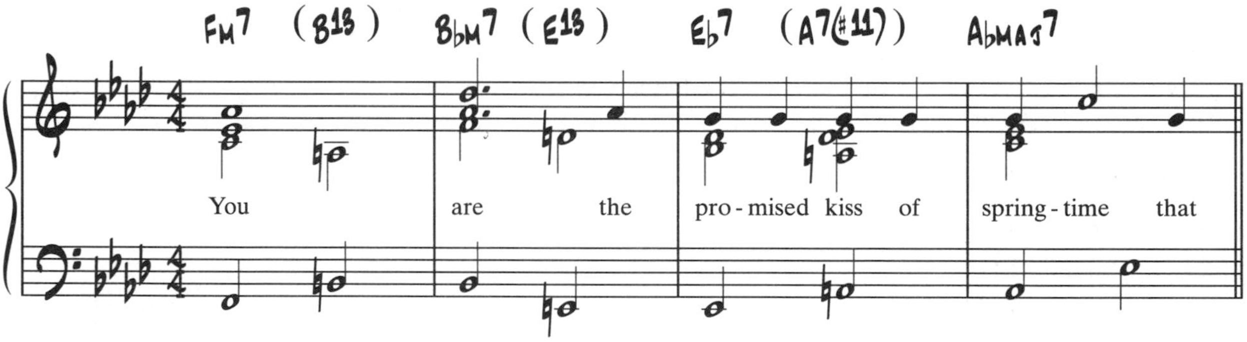

Relative Major/Minor Substitution
Quite simply, it's where a major chord is replaced by its relative minor. Conversely, the minor chord can be replaced by its relative major.

Becomes:

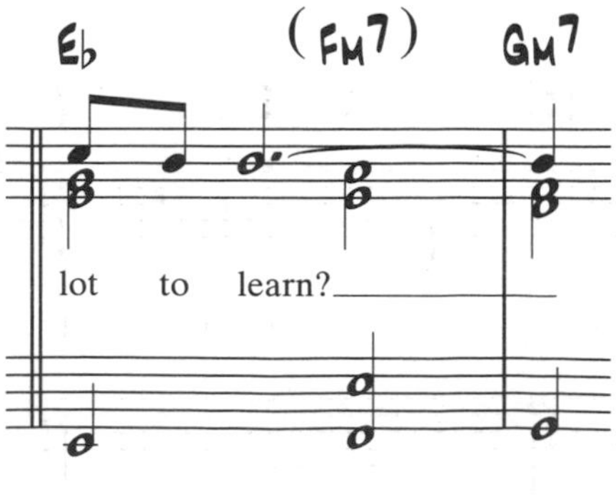

V7 Substitution

oically, it's where a II-V7 turnaround is substituted for the V7 chord alone. (This also works great at the end of a chorus when ı wish to repeat back to its beginning.)

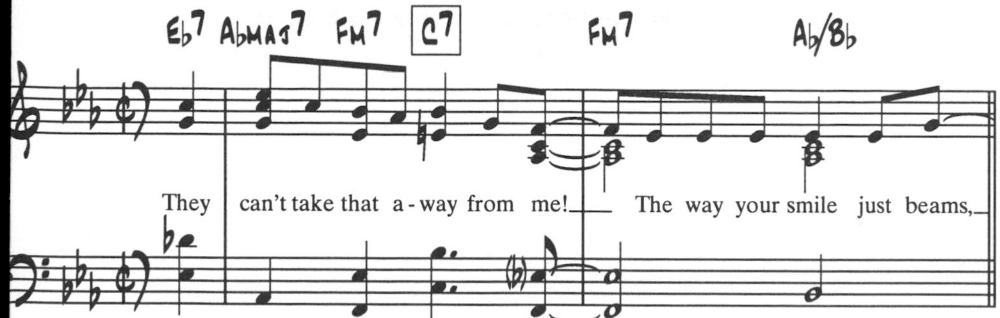

Becomes:

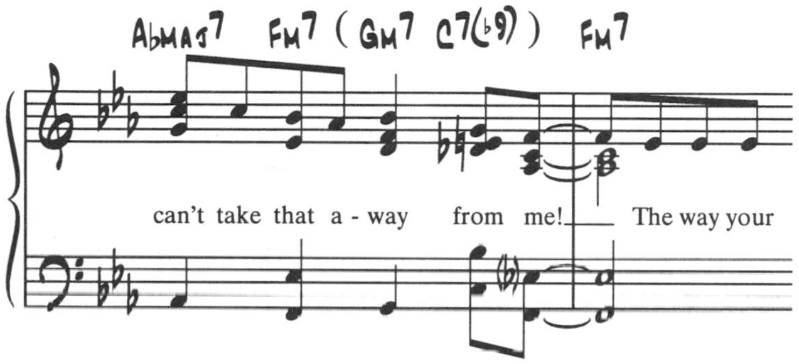

ajor/Minor Substitution

metimes, simply changing a chord from a minor to major tonality (and vice versa) will provide an interesting variation. Using ; same musical example shown above, let's substitute a major chord for the last minor chord displayed.

hromatic Substitution

; where an ascending or descending chromatic chordal pattern is substituted for the original phrase.

becomes

CHORD THEORY

Chord theory

All chords are built from the major scale. **You can figure out the notes in any major scale by applying this pattern of whole- and half-steps: W W H W W W H.**

For example, the A major scale:

A		B		C♯		D		E		F♯		G♯		A
	W		W		H		W		W		W		H	

The scale tones can be numbered:

A	B	C♯	D	E	F♯	G♯	A	B	C♯	D	E	F♯
1	2	3	4	5	6	7	8	9	10	11	12	13

Any chord can be built from its corresponding major scale by applying the appropriate chord pattern.

Chord Patterns		**Examples (Key of A)**	
Major:	1 3 5	A:	A C♯ E
Minor:	1 ♭3 5	Am:	A C E
Dominant 7:	1 3 5 ♭7	A7:	A C♯ E G
Major 7:	1 3 5 7	Amaj7:	A C♯ E G♯
Major 6:	1 3 5 6	A6:	A C♯ E F♯
Minor 7:	1 ♭3 5 ♭7	Am7:	A C E G
Add 9:	1 3 5 9	A(9):	A C♯ E B
Suspended 4:	1 4 5	Asus:	A D E
Dominant 9:	1 3 5 ♭7 9	A9:	A C♯ E G B
Dominant 13:	1 3 5 ♭7 13	A13:	A C♯ E G F♯
Dominant 7(♭9):	1 3 5 ♭7 ♭9	A7(♭9):	A C♯ E G B♭
Minor 9:	1 ♭3 5 9	Am9:	A C E B
Minor 7(♭5):	1 ♭3 ♭5 ♭7	Am7(♭5):	A C E♭ G
Diminished 7:	1 ♭3 ♭5 ♭♭7*(6)	A°7:	A C E♭ F♯
Augmented:	1 3 ♯5	A+:	A C♯ E♯
Dominant 7(♯5):	1 3 ♯5 ♭7	A7(♯5):	A C♯ E♯ G
Dominant 7(♯9):	1 3 5 ♭7 ♯9**(♭3)	A7(♯9):	A C♯ E G C♮

* ♭♭7 = 6
** ♯9 = ♭3

The *Just Standards Real Book* features 250 classic standards. These songs form core repertoire for all musicians the world over.

AFTER YOU
AIN'T MISBEHAVIN'
AIN'T SHE SWEET
AL DI LA
ALICE IN WONDERLAND
ALL OF YOU
ALL OR NOTHING AT ALL
ALL THE THINGS YOU ARE
ALL THE WAY
ALL THROUGH THE NIGHT
ALMOST LIKE BEING IN LOVE
AM I BLUE
ANYTHING GOES
APRIL IN PARIS
AS TIME GOES BY
AT LAST
AT LONG LAST LOVE
A-TISKET, A-TASKET
AUTUMN IN NEW YORK
BE A CLOWN
BEGIN THE BEGUINE
BEI MIR BIST DU SCHON
BESS, YOU IS MY WOMAN NOW
THE BEST IS YET TO COME
THE BEST THINGS IN LIFE ARE FREE
BETWEEN THE DEVIL AND THE DEEP BLUE SEA
BEWITCHED (Bothered and Bewildered)
BIDIN' MY TIME
BILL BAILEY, WON'T YOU PLEASE COME HOME?
BIRTH OF THE BLUES
BLUE MOON
THE BLUE ROOM
BLUES IN THE NIGHT (My Mama Done Tol' Me)
BODY AND SOUL
BOOGIE WOOGIE BUGLE BOY
THE BOULEVARD OF BROKEN DREAMS
BUT NOT FOR ME
BYE, BYE, BLACKBIRD
CANDY
CAN'T HELP LOVIN' DAT MAN
CHARADE
CHERRY PINK AND APPLE BLOSSOM WHITE
COME BLOW YOUR HORN
COME FLY WITH ME
COME RAIN OR COME SHINE
CRY ME A RIVER
DANCING IN THE DARK
DANCING ON THE CEILING
DAY IN, DAY OUT
DAY IN THE LIFE OF A FOOL
DAYS OF WINE AND ROSES
DEEP PURPLE
DO NOTHIN' TILL YOU HEAR FROM ME
(Sittin' On) THE DOCK OF THE BAY
DON'T BLAME ME
DON'T CRY FOR ME ARGENTINA
DON'T FENCE ME IN
DON'T GET AROUND MUCH ANYMORE
EAST OF THE SUN (And West of the Moon)
EASY TO LOVE
EBB TIDE
EMBRACEABLE YOU
EMILY
EVERGREEN (Love Theme From "A Star Is Born")
EVERYTHING MUST CHANGE
FALLING IN LOVE WITH LOVE
FASCINATIN' RHYTHM
A FINE ROMANCE
FIVE FOOT TWO, EYES OF BLUE
A FOGGY DAY
(I Love You) FOR SENTIMENTAL REASONS
FORTY-SECOND STREET
FROM A DISTANCE
FROSTY THE SNOWMAN
GEE BABY, AIN'T I BEEN GOOD TO YOU
THE GIRL FROM IPANEMA
GOLDFINGER
THE GOOD LIFE
THE GREATEST LOVE OF ALL
HAPPY DAYS ARE HERE AGAIN
HAVE YOU MET MISS JONES
HAVE YOURSELF A MERRY LITTLE CHRISTMAS
HEY THERE
HIGH NOON (Do Not Forsake Me)
HOLD ME, THRILL ME, KISS ME
HOW ABOUT YOU?
HOW HIGH THE MOON
HOW INSENSITIVE
HOW LITTLE WE KNOW
I CAN'T GET STARTED
I CAN'T GIVE YOU ANYTHING BUT LOVE
I CONCENTRATE ON YOU
I COULD HAVE DANCED ALL NIGHT
I COULD WRITE A BOOK
I COVER THE WATERFRONT
I DIDN'T KNOW ABOUT YOU
I DIDN'T KNOW WHAT TIME IT WAS
I GET A KICK OUT OF YOU
I GOT RHYTHM
I HAD THE CRAZIEST DREAM
I LET A SONG GO OUT OF MY HEART
I LOVE PARIS
I LOVES YOU PORGY
I ONLY HAVE EYES FOR YOU
I REMEMBER IT WELL
I THOUGHT ABOUT YOU
I WANNA BE AROUND (To Pick Up the Pieces)
I WILL WAIT FOR YOU
I WISH I KNEW
I WISH YOU LOVE
I WON'T DANCE
IF EVER I WOULD LEAVE YOU
I'LL REMEMBER APRIL
I'LL SEE YOU IN MY DREAMS
I'M IN THE MOOD FOR LOVE
I'M THRU WITH LOVE
IN A SENTIMENTAL MOOD
IN THE STILL OF THE NIGHT
IS YOU IS OR IS YOU AIN'T (Ma Baby)
IT AIN'T NECESSARILY SO
IT HAD TO BE YOU
IT WAS A VERY GOOD YEAR
IT'S BEEN A LONG, LONG TIME
IT'S ONLY A PAPER MOON
I'VE GOT A CRUSH ON YOU
I'VE GOT THE WORLD ON A STRING
I'VE GOT YOU UNDER MY SKIN
I'VE GROWN ACCUSTOMED TO HER FACE
THE JAMES BOND THEME
JINGLE BELL ROCK
JUST A GIGOLO
JUST IN TIME
JUST ONE OF THOSE THINGS
LA VIE EN ROSE
THE LADY IS A TRAMP
LAURA
LET IT SNOW! LET IT SNOW! LET IT SNOW!
LET'S CALL THE WHOLE THING OFF
LET'S DO IT (Let's Fall in Love)
LI'L DARLIN'
LIMEHOUSE BLUES
LITTLE BOY LOST (Pieces of Dreams)
THE LITTLE DRUMMER BOY
LOVE FOR SALE
LOVE IS A MANY-SPLENDORED THING
LOVE IS HERE TO STAY
LOVER MAN
LULLABY OF BROADWAY
MACK THE KNIFE
A MAN AND A WOMAN
THE MAN I LOVE
THE MAN THAT GOT AWAY
MEDITATION
MISTY
MOMENT TO MOMENT
MOONGLOW
MOONLIGHT IN VERMONT
MOONLIGHT SERENADE
THE MORE I SEE YOU
MORE THAN YOU KNOW
MOUNTAIN GREENERY
MY FUNNY VALENTINE
MY KIND OF TOWN (Chicago Is)
MY WAY
NEVER ON SUNDAY
NEVERTHELESS (I'm in Love With You)
NEW YORK, NEW YORK (On the Town)
NICE WORK IF YOU CAN GET IT
NIGHT AND DAY
ON THE STREET WHERE YOU LIVE
ONCE IN A WHILE
OVER THE RAINBOW
THE PARTY'S OVER
PENNIES FROM HEAVEN
PEOPLE
THE PINK PANTHER
PRELUDE TO A KISS
QUANDO QUANDO QUANDO (Tell Me When)
QUIET NIGHTS OF QUIET STARS (Corcovado)
ROCK-A-BYE YOUR BABY WITH A DIXIE MELODY
'S WONDERFUL
SATIN DOLL
THE SECOND TIME AROUND
SECRET LOVE
SEND IN THE CLOWNS
SEPTEMBER IN THE RAIN
SEPTEMBER OF MY YEARS
SEPTEMBER SONG
THE SHADOW OF YOUR SMILE
SHE'S FUNNY THAT WAY
SINCE I FELL FOR YOU
SKYLARK
SLEIGH RIDE
SLOW HOT WIND
SMALL WORLD
SMOKE GETS IN YOUR EYES
SOFTLY AS I LEAVE YOU
SOFTLY, AS IN A MORNNG SUNRISE
SOMEONE TO WATCH OVER ME
SOMEWHERE MY LOVE (Lara's Theme From "Dr. Zhivago
THE SONG IS YOU
SPEAK LOW
STARDUST
STARS FELL ON ALABAMA
STRANGERS IN THE NIGHT
SUMMER WIND
SUMMERTIME
A SUNDAY KIND OF LOVE
SUNNY
SWEET GEORGIA BROWN
TAIN'T NOBODY'S BUSINESS (If
TAKING A CHANCE ON LOVE
TEA FOR TWO
TEACH ME TONIGHT
TEMPTATION
THAT'S LIFE
THEME FROM "A SUMMER PLA
THEME FROM NEW YORK, NEW YORK (Start Spreading the News
THERE'S A SMALL HOTEL
THEY CAN'T TAKE THAT AWAY FROM ME
THUNDERBALL
TOO MARVELOUS FOR WORDS
TOOT, TOOT, TOOTSIE! (Goodbye)
TRY TO REMEMBER
TWO FOR THE ROAD
WATCH WHAT HAPPENS
THE WAY YOU LOOK TONIGHT
WE'VE ONLY JUST BEGUN
WHAT A WONDERFUL WORLD
WHAT ARE YOU DOING THE RES OF YOUR LIFE?
WHAT IS THIS THING CALLED LOVE?
WHAT'S NEW?
WHEN I FALL IN LOVE
WHEN YOU'RE SMILING (The Whole World Smiles With Yo
WHERE OR WHEN
WHO'S SORRY NOW?
WHY CAN'T I
WILLOW WEEP FOR ME
THE WIND BENEATH MY WINGS
WINTER WONDERLAND
WITCHCRAFT
WITH A SONG IN MY HEART
YESTERDAYS
YOU ARE SO BEAUTIFUL
YOU DO SOMETHING TO ME
YOU GO TO MY HEAD
YOU LIGHT UP MY LIFE
YOU MAKE ME FEEL SO YOUNG
YOU MUST HAVE BEEN A BEAUTIFUL BABY
YOU STEPPED OUT OF A DREAM